Your Towns and Cities in tl

Maidstone
in the Great War

Your Towns and Cities in the Great War

Maidstone
in the Great War

Stephen Wynn

Pen & Sword
MILITARY

First published in Great Britain in 2017 by
PEN & SWORD MILITARY
an imprint of
Pen and Sword Books Ltd
47 Church Street
Barnsley
South Yorkshire S70 2AS

ISBN 978 1 47382 791 2

Printed and bound in England
by CPI Group (UK) Ltd, Croydon, CR0 4YY

Typeset in Times New Roman by Chic Graphics

Pen & Sword Books Ltd incorporates the imprints of
Pen & Sword Archaeology, Atlas, Aviation, Battleground, Discovery,
Family History, History, Maritime, Military, Naval, Politics, Railways,
Select, Social History, Transport, True Crime, Claymore Press,
Frontline Books, Leo Cooper, Praetorian Press, Remember When,
Seaforth Publishing and Wharncliffe.

For a complete list of Pen and Sword titles please contact
Pen and Sword Books Limited
47 Church Street, Barnsley, South Yorkshire, S70 2AS, England
E-mail: enquiries@pen-and-sword.co.uk
Website: www.pen-and-sword.co.uk

Contents

Author's Biography

Stephen is a happily retired police officer who served with Essex Police as a constable for thirty years between 1983 and 2013. He is married to Tanya who is also his best friend.

Both his sons, Luke and Ross, were members of the armed forces, collectively serving five tours of Afghanistan between 2008 and 2013. Both were injured on their first tour. This led to his first book, *Two Sons in a Warzone – Afghanistan: The True Story of a Father's Conflict*, which was published in October 2010.

Both of his grandfathers served in and survived the First World War, one with the Royal Irish Rifles, the other in the Mercantile Navy, while his father was a member of the Royal Army Ordinance Corps during the Second World War.

His teenage daughter, Aimee, currently attends a local secondary school.

Stephen collaborated with Ken Porter on a previous book published in August 2012, *German POW Camp 266 – Langdon Hills*. It spent six weeks as the number one best-selling book in Waterstones, Basildon, between March and April 2013. They have also collaborated on four books in the Towns & Cities in the Great War series by Pen and Sword. Stephen has also written other titles in the same series.

Stephen has also co-written three crime thrillers which were published between 2010 and 2012 and centre around a fictional detective named Terry Danvers.

When he is not writing, Tanya and he enjoy the simplicity of walking their four German shepherd dogs early each morning when most sensible people are still fast asleep in their beds.

CHAPTER 1

General History of Maidstone

Maidstone has a long and varied history going back to Mesolithic times, but it was the Romans who really played a significant part in making the town what it is today. They routed Watling Street, between Rochester and Hastings, through Maidstone, which greatly improved its trading capabilities and put it well and truly on the map. Watling Street, which was an ancient trackway, stretched from the Kent coast, carried on through London and St. Albans, and continued all the way through to Wales.

After the Battle of Hastings and the Norman invasion in 1066, the Norman influence throughout the country, Kent in particular, increased drastically.

The Archbishop's Palace, which dates back to the fourteenth century, and which still stands today, sits on the banks of the River Medway. It was here in 1381 during the Peasants Revolt that the radical preacher John Ball, having been arrested, was detained by the then Archbishop, Chancellor Sudbury. He was freed on 11 June 1381 by Wat Tyler's peasant army as they made their way to London. Ball's freedom was to be short lived. He was arrested in Coventry and put on trial at St. Albans on 15 July 1381 in front of King Richard ll, found guilty, and for his punishment was hung, drawn and quartered.

Thomas Hilton is considered by many to be the first English Protestant martyr of the Reformation. Hilton was a priest with a different interpretation of Catholicism from that which had been laid down as doctrine by the Catholic Church in Rome. He had been hiding out in Europe with other members of his group when, in 1529, he made his way back to England to meet up with his supporters. On attempting to leave England again, he was detained at Gravesend. Because of letters found in his possession, he was arrested on the grounds of heresy, interrogated, put on trial and found guilty as charged. He was burnt at the stake in Maidstone on 23 February 1530.

In Maidstone in 1557, William and Katherine Allin, who were Protestants, committed the heinous offences of reading the scriptures to the common people, feeding the poor and selling corn at half price. 'A small fine?' I hear you say, or maybe put to the town's stocks to have rotting fruit and vegetables thrown at them? No. Along with five other Protestants, they were burnt at the stake as part of the Marian Persecutions, a drive against Protestant religious reformers.

On 1 June 1648 the Battle of Maidstone took place during the Second English Civil War which resulted in a victory for the Parliamentarians who, under the command of Sir Thomas Fairfax, had amassed some 4,000 veteran troops to march on the town. The battle raged for most of the day in atrocious weather. Despite a stout and heroic defence of the town in which over 800 Royalists perished, those who were still alive surrendered just after midnight. They were subsequently released to return home to their families.

In 1797, with countries across Europe falling under control of the ever-advancing armies of Napoleon 1 of France, the threat of a French invasion, was very real. As was a common theme throughout Britain at the time, most towns, or at least the ones who could afford to, raised a local militia which could be called on in a time of military need. Maidstone had two barracks built, the first of which went on to become the home of the West Kent Regiment. The other barracks, which were built along the Sandling Road, went on to become an Army riding school.

In 1799, 3,000 troops from the Kent Volunteers assembled in Maidstone's Mote Park and were inspected by King George lll and his

Prime Minister William Pitt in an effort to gauge the readiness of the country's preparations in the event of a French invasion.

In 1819 Maidstone prison was completed, although the first inmates had already taken up residency there in the latter months of 1818. It was constructed by French prisoners of war. Fifty years after its opening it became somewhat notorious as the place of the execution of Frances Kidder, the last woman to be hung in public in Britain, on 2 April 1868. She had been convicted of murdering her stepdaughter Louisa Kidder-Staples by drowning her in a ditch. She was hung outside the gaol at noon by William Cathcart in front of a crowd of some 2,000 people, including her husband.

Maidstone has had quite an involvement in military matters over the years, so an influx of young men in uniform when the First World War broke out was nothing new to the local people. They simply did what they had always done at such times, they embraced the moment as best they could.

CHAPTER 2

1914
Starting Out

The rumblings of war in Europe had finally come to fruition on 4 August 1914 when Great Britain declared war on Germany after she had invaded Belgium and refused to leave

Although only five months of the war were in 1914, an amazing thirty-seven battles took place. In that time a total of 37,621 British and Commonwealth soldiers were killed. This included 152 men from The Buffs (East Kent Regiment) and 285 from the Queen's Own (Royal West Kent Regiment). Both regiments would have included men from Maidstone.

The war immediately began to affect all aspects of society and everyday life. On Thursday, 6 August, with the war just two days old, Messrs Lambert & Symes, estate agents from Paddock Wood, were holding an auction at the Star Hotel in Maidstone of three properties which they owned. Only one of the properties sold: Ivy House in Ditton, which sold to Mr Henry George Henbrey from Maidstone for £345. Laddingford Lodge at Yalding did not receive a single bid, and Yew Lodge at Laddington was withdrawn by the auctioneer when it failed to reach its reserve price.

Mr Henbrey, the purchaser of Ivy House, was by profession an auctioneer. At the time of his death on 23 November 1949 he was living at 24 King Street, Maidstone, so whether he purchased Ivy House to live in or as a postwar investment is not known.

The lack of sales was due in the main to concerns about the war and how property would be affected if the Germans invaded Great Britain. The auctioneer was moved to say that if people imagined the war would make any difference to the value of English property, they were mistaken. He went on to say that 'English property was the best protected in the world', and he expected a great revival in the value of property once the war was over, making property an excellent long term investment.

The following incident took place within a matter of days of the start of the war. It involved Sergeant (1141) Henry Belcher of the 1st/1st Battalion Surrey Yeomanry (Queen Mary's Regiment) who was stationed at Maidstone. He had enlisted on 20 March 1908 at Upton-on-Severn in Worcester, having been a farrier by trade. It was initially reported that he had been attacked by a German spy, which understandably caused somewhat of a sensation throughout Maidstone. Sergeant Belcher had sustained a stab wound to the throat which had apparently been caused by a service knife. It later transpired that he had been suffering from depression. Sergeant Belcher died of his wounds two months later on 10 November 1914. He is buried at Netley Military Cemetery near Southampton. He was most likely transferred from hospital in Maidstone to the Royal Victoria Military Hospital at Netley, where he died. Netley had a psychiatric unit which later dealt with men who returned from the war suffering from shell shock.

On 10 August 1914, less than a week after the outbreak of war, a meeting was held at the Sessions House in Maidstone. It had been called by the Lord Lieutenant of Kent, the Marquis of Camden, and its purpose was to discuss Lord Kitchener's appeal for 100,000 recruits to enlist in the British Army. The meeting was well attended by the county's great and good; there were Members of Parliament, senior military personnel, peers and knights of the realm, councillors, the Mayor of Maidstone Mr A.T. Epps, and other ordinary gentlemen who had neither military nor noble titles to their names. The meeting was chaired by Mr Cornwallis who started by reading out a letter from the Lord Lieutenant expressing his regret that he was unable to attend the meeting himself because of his own military commitments with the West Kent Yeomanry. The letter continued by explaining that the Lord Lieutenant had opened a subscription list for Kent on behalf of the Prince of Wales National Relief Fund and that he would greatly appreciate it if those in charge of the large boroughs and districts would assist. It is not recorded if anybody refused the Lord Lieutenant's request.

Mr Cornwallis then read further from the letter, in which the Lord Lieutenant had written that he attached the greatest importance and saw it as his immediate duty to bring to the notice of the county's young men, who were between 18 and 30 years of age, the urgency and importance of assisting Lord Kitchener in his appeal for 100,000 men to enlist.

Major Wood Martyn, an Army representative, informed the meeting that when he was asked to attend, he thought that he might take the opportunity to pay a visit to the West Kent's Depot Regiment to see how things were going. When he did so he discovered two officers present from the local Territorial Force but that all of the regular officers had left to go to the front. He further reported that there were seven Army pensioners employed to undertake recruitment-related work, but to effectively cover an area the size of Maidstone they would need more like seventy men to do the job. Major Wood Martyn suggested to the meeting that in his opinion the quickest and most effective way to obtain recruits was to strengthen the recruiting sub-committees and to have meetings in villages as well as the bigger towns. They also needed to pay Army pensioners in Canterbury and Maidstone Depots to do a leaflet drop door to door to make young men aware of the locations of the recruiting offices.

Mr H.W. Forster MP then moved the following resolution: 'That this meeting pledges itself to use its utmost endeavour to encourage recruiting of all those eligible men to serve in response to the appeal for 100,000 men made by Lord Kitchener, Secretary of State for War, and urges every district to take immediate steps to make the appeal known to young men in its area.'

Lord Harris seconded the resolution, and there followed an exchange between Mr Forster and Lord Harris about what constituted the best outcome. In his keenness to expedite matters concerning the recruiting process and how best it could operate, Mr Forster made comment that although he did not wish to dictate to others how best they could obtain recruits, he could only tell them what he was going to do. It was his intention to ask his political opponents to join him and unite their political organisations to obtain recruits and then transfer them to the recruiting depots. As politicians they already had 'machinery' in place in every village which could be speedily set in motion at a moment's notice. He recognized that others might have other methods and ideas on this point, but pointed out if they were going spend some days in creating machinery, this was going to take time and time was of the essence.

Up stepped Lord Harris with his view on the matter. He asked Mr Forster if it would not be better to utilize the existing machinery of the Territorial Association for the purpose of obtaining recruits. 'After all,' he said, 'the association was far more expert on the matter of recruitment than any particular political party could ever possibly be, and they would be able to do the work much more effectively and efficiently.'

Mr Forster then clarified his position and stated that he had no desire or intention of turning any premises or organisations in his constituency into recruiting offices, but merely advertising agencies for the purpose of recruitment.

The Mayor of Maidstone, Councillor A.T. Epps, then moved 'that all present will do their utmost to support Lord Kitchener's appeal for the Kent War Relief Fund by opening local subscription lists.' The Mayor's motion was seconded and passed.

In the early days of the war there was an enthusiasm for people of every social class to do whatever they could for the war effort.

On 15 August 1914 a meeting took place in Maidstone to coordinate Kent's wartime voluntary organisations in an attempt at ensuring their effective and productive use. This involved the local Territorial Army, the Red Cross Society, the St. John Ambulance Society and the Voluntary Aid Detachment. If not properly coordinated, their efforts could become unintentionally duplicated and therefore counter-productive. It was with this in mind that the Kent Voluntary Aid

Organisation was formed to centralize and unify all such groups. The county-wide director of the new group was Doctor Cotton, with Doctor Yolland as the chief staff officer who, in the absence of Lord Sackville, also had to perform the roles of Hon Treasurer and Hon Secretary.

All of the organisations who were part of the group had, in preparation for an anticipated war, already started forming, enlarging and training their personnel so that they would be able to take an active part on the home front when required to do so. The members of all of these organisations gave their time and energies freely, managing to fit in all of their other daily commitments around their voluntary work.

The Marchioness of Camden was appointed as the President of the Kent Voluntary Aid Organisation.

The *Kent & Sussex Courier* of 21 August contained a section entitled 'Maidstone War Items'. The first item was as follows:

> *A squadron of the Surrey (Queen Mary's Own) Yeomanry, which is stationed at Maidstone, is billeted with Mr F S W Cornwallis, at Linton Road.*

This relates to Mr Fiennes Stanley Wykeham Cornwallis, who lived at Linton Park, Maidstone, with his wife Mabel, their daughters, Julia, Yvonne, and Bridget, as well as twenty servants of different descriptions. They lived in a massive house which was why they needed so many servants and why they were able to billet a squadron of military men in their midst. The estate of 330 acres is still privately owned and is not open to the public.

Other items in that section were as follows:

> *2,000 troops, which comprised men from the 1st, 4th and 5th Battalions of the Royal West Surrey (The Queen's) as well as elements of the 5th and 6th Battalions, East Surrey Regiment, were also billeted in the town.*

> *Maidstone Girls Grammar School was guarded by two light machine guns.*

Postcard of 1906 Linton Park Maidstone, home of the Cornwallis family.

The Bridge was guarded on each side by armed sentries, who patrolled it day and night.

It is quite a familiar sight in Maidstone to see men armed with rifles and bayonets, and the changing of the various guards at the respective headquarters has now become time worn.

Sir Marcus Samuel of the Mote House, Maidstone, has equipped and will maintain a hospital at his house for military and naval officers.

The former stately home of Mote House sits in 450 acres of land which today is a public park. The original Mote House was demolished sometime around 1800 and the current structure built in its place. The estate was sold to Marcus Samuel, the 1st Viscount Bearsted, in 1895.

General hospitals have been scheduled at Hayle Place in Maidstone and the Howard de Walden Institute,

*Maidstone, for the sick and wounded soldiers. The latter
hospital is ready to receive patients now, and Hayle Place,
will be ready by the close of the week.*

The Howard de Walden Institute hospital was named after its
benefactor Lord Howard de Walden. Hayle Place was a VAD
convalescent hospital to where soldiers were often transferred from
general hospitals after their injuries or wounds had been sufficiently
treated.

The Defence of the Realm Act (DORA) made it an offence for
anybody to walk around the streets of Maidstone carrying a camera.
Anybody caught taking photographs, especially of any military
personnel or barracks, would have found themselves in serious trouble,
facing either a hefty fine or an allegation of being a spy at the worst.

As of Friday, 21 August 1914, all licensed public houses within
Maidstone were required to close an hour early each evening, meaning
that last orders would be at ten o'clock and not at eleven. This came
about as a result of a request by the local military authorities to the
Licensing Committee of the Maidstone Borough Magistrates to put in
place such an order. As the clubs in the same area were not legally
compelled by the magistrate's order it was suggested that the
committees of the various clubs should be 'persuaded' to close their
bars at the same time. How it was realistically expected for that to be
achieved was not made clear.

On Sunday, 23 August 1914, a religious service was held at Foley
Park in Maidstone that was attended by the Surrey Infantry Brigade
which comprised the Queen's Royal West Surrey Regiment along with
the 5th and 6th Battalions of the East Surrey Regiment. In overall
command of the event was the recently promoted, Brigadier General
Marriot MVO DSO. Reports of the day describe it as a 'wonderful
service, a service to grip the heart and to set in vibrant play the deepest
chords of our common humanity'. The service was given by the
Reverend E.C. Kirwan who was the Vicar of Holy Trinity and St.
Mary's Parish church in Guildford. He was also the Army Chaplain to
the 5th Battalion, the Queen's. Looking resplendent he stood on the
open back of a lorry, gracefully accompanied by Lieutenant Chadwyck-

Healey on the piano who played a selection of the nation's best-known and well-loved hymns. Those present were some four thousand in number. The choir consisted of military personnel in its entirety, officers and men, and stood slightly to the front of Reverend Kirwan; sadly there was no band. The hymns were *Eternal Father, Strong to Save*, *O God our Help in Ages Past*, and *Jesu, Lover of my Soul*. At the end of his sermon Reverend Kirwan made special mention of British soldiers and sailors, the sick and wounded, doctors and nurses, along with the fatherless and widows. With each of the vicar's words came a clearer picture of the horrors and sadness of the war. The service ended with a rousing rendition of the national anthem.

The end of August saw a lot of activity in Maidstone with troops coming and going as men prepared and readied themselves for war. The week commencing Monday, 24 August, had everybody on their toes. It was a week of sudden and surprise alarms ringing at odd hours of the day and night to let men in Maidstone know that their units were being readied to leave the town.

The Surrey Regiment received their alarm call on Tuesday evening at about 8.30 pm. The men, whether in their billets, the local theatre, or the cinema (or picture palace as it was called back then), ran as swiftly as they could back to their company headquarters. The mobilization went ahead in a speedy fashion: the complete column of men was on the march within fifteen minutes of the alarm having been sounded. In the early hours of the following morning it was the turn of the Surrey Yeomanry to receive their surprise alarm.

On Wednesday evening an urgent appeal was made by Lord Hythe of the Queen's Own West Kent Yeomanry for more men to join the regiment to get them up to full strength as they prepared themselves for foreign service. Those who wanted to enlist in the Yeomanry had to do so in person at the Regimental Depot in Union Street, Maidstone, the following day. The Maidstone element of the regiment was 'D' Squadron. The men who served in the Yeomanry did so voluntarily as it was a Territorial Unit and as such they were only ever intended to be used for home service and could not be forced to serve outside the country. At the outbreak of the war some members made it be known that they were happy to serve in foreign theatres of war. The Territorials were to be split into 1st and 2nd line units. The 1st line were men who had volunteered for overseas service, while the latter were those who couldn't serve overseas because of other commitments, or simply because they didn't want to. The appeal was a success, with more than thirty suitable young men presenting themselves as requested.

By the end of the war thirty-seven young men had been killed while serving with the West Kent Yeomanry, nineteen of them in just one day on 31 August 1916. The first man to be killed was Captain Bertrand Stewart who was 42 years of age and who at the time of his death on 14 September 1914 was attached to the Intelligence Corps. The last man of the Yeomanry to be killed died on 5 September 1916. He was Private 2515 J.S. Turner of the 3rd/1st Battalion and is buried at St. Sever Cemetery in Rouen.

Thursday, 27 August, saw two battalions of the East Surrey Regiment leave Maidstone, followed the next day by the entire Surrey Infantry Brigade, along with elements of the West Surrey Regiment, who undertook their journey on foot. By nightfall they had made it as far as Charing, where they camped for the night before continuing on their way the following morning.

As September arrived Maidstone was a hive of activity. The following article appeared in the *Kent & Sussex Courier* newspaper dated Friday, 11 September 1914:

The West Kent Yeomanry

Those NCOs and men of the West Kent Yeomanry who did not volunteer for foreign service have now returned to Maidstone and are billeted in the Union Street Council School. They will form the nucleus of a Depot for the West Kent Yeomanry, which, we understand, is now up to strength and ready to be despatched to some foreign military station, where they will relieve one of the regular cavalry regiments. It is stated that their destination is to be Cairo where the 21st Lancers are at present stationed.

By the end of the First World War a total of eighty-one members of the 21st Lancers had been killed.

In the same edition of the newspaper there was a story about a Lance Corporal Clarke of Yalding, whose parents lived in Maidstone. He was wounded during the fighting at the Battle of Mons and sent back to Britain where he was treated at Netley Military Hospital. After treatment he was well enough to be discharged from the hospital and sent to stay with his parents in Maidstone. Before the outbreak of hostilities, he was based with his Battalion in Dublin and they sailed from there to Le Havre where the locals gave them a wonderful reception on their arrival, providing them with gifts of food, fruit, cigarettes and wine. He spoke about how the French people referred to the British soldiers as 'those brave English'. There was little time for festivities as Lance Corporal Clarke and his colleagues soon found themselves on a French transport train heading for an unknown destination, with the cheers of the French people ringing in their ears. Next they arrived at Mons, of which most of them would never have heard, and then discovered that they had a day's march before reaching their allocated destination. As soon as they arrived they began digging and preparing defensive trenches, but before they had got anywhere near finishing, the Germans began an artillery bombardment. Lance Corporal Clarke and the men under his charge were fortunate to have had the shelter of a farm house wall that provided them with an element of safety from the shells that were exploding all around. Their position was attacked for some fifteen hours, during which Clarke and his men managed steadily to pick off the Germans with effective and accurate rifle fire. But the Germans continued their assault with overwhelming strength of numbers, and their advance was not checked. Once the decision had been taken for British troops to begin their retreat from Mons, the West Kents were set the task of forming a rearguard action to allow the main body of men to make good their escape from a rapidly advancing German Army. It wasn't quite a suicide mission, but their chances of survival were slim at best. It was during this fighting that Clarke was struck in the left leg by a fragment of shrapnel and due to a combination of pain and shock he was rendered unconscious. When he came round he discovered that he was minus his rifle and ammunition and assumed that the Germans who overran his position thought that he was dead and removed his equipment from him. It is believed that while Clarke was unconscious, some of his wounded colleagues were bayoneted by the Germans. Eventually, when he had recovered enough to get to his feet, he was joined by another wounded comrade who had survived and together they escaped, but they still had to be careful, as German Uhlans were riding through the dead and wounded British lying all around. Clarke and his unknown colleague eventually found their way to a British Red Cross wagon that took them to a nearby building which was being used as a hospital. Despite a large visible Red Cross flag outside the building, the Germans were raining down artillery shells on it. Other wounded colleagues of Clarke would later tell similar stories, confirming incidents of hospital stations and even a nunnery where the sisters were tending to wounded soldiers being struck by German shells. Whether the Germans knew that the buildings they were bombarding were being used as hospitals is not known. Moments after Clarke had left the hospital, the roof of the building was blown off by a German shell. He was taken to Le Havre where he was put on a British hospital ship and sent back to England where he was taken initially to Woolwich Military Hospital and then to Maidstone Hospital to fully recuperate.

There was one report of advancing German infantry coming across a wounded British soldier, named only as Colour Sergeant Saunders, while he was being carried on a stretcher. It is reported that he was bayoneted by the Germans. A check on the Commonwealth War Graves Commission website records that Colour Sergeant (L/4607) W.B. Saunders of the 1st Battalion, Queen's Own (Royal West Kent Regiment) was killed in action on 24 August 1914 and is buried at the Military Cemetery in the Belgian village of Hautrage, fifteen kilometres west of Mons. A further check of the British Army's First World War medal rolls index shows Colour Sergeant (4607) Walter B. Saunders of the Queen's Own (Royal West Kent Regiment) who had first arrived in Belgium on 15 August 1914 and who was killed in action just nine days later on 24 August 1914.

Other members of the West Kents who were at Maidstone Hospital with Clarke had written letters home to their loved ones. Some of them were included in an article which appeared in the *Kent & Sussex*

Courier on Friday, 11 September 1914. An unnamed Private of the West Kents wrote the following about what he had witnessed:

> *Just when the firing ceased a little, we got the order to fire at their infantry. A flock of sheep, 2,000 or 3,000 in number, trying to rush out of a field, was nothing compared to the hordes of Germans. They were all cut to smithereens, but as we mowed them down, others flocked in larger numbers and took their places.*

A wounded corporal wrote:

> *It looked as if we were going to be snowed under. The mass of men that came at us was an avalanche, and every one of us must have been simply trodden to death and not killed by bullets or shells when our Cavalry charged in to them on the left wing, not 500 yards from the trench I was in, and cut them up. Our lads did the rest, but the shells afterwards laid low a lot of them.*

Another West Kent private wrote a letter to his father:

> *You complained last year of the swarms of wasps that destroyed your fruit. Well, dad, they were certainly no larger in number than the Germans who came for us.*
>
> *The Germans are cowards when they get the bayonets at them. A young Lieutenant, I don't know his name, was one of the coolest men I have ever seen, and didn't he encourage our chaps! I saw him bring down a couple of Germans who were leading half a company of men.*

In the early weeks of the war, with wounded British soldiers returning home, such stories were becoming more and more common. Added to the sight of wounded and disabled British soldiers, some who had lost limbs, either in explosions or by amputation, the war suddenly became very real indeed.

In the same edition of the newspaper was the story of Major Pack-Beresford who was wounded while serving in Belgium during the early weeks of the war. Between 1911 and the outbreak of the First World War, he had been in command of the Maidstone Depot of the Queen's Own (Royal West Kent Regiment). He was regarded by many of his peers as well as most of the common soldiery as being an ideal commander. At his last speech, which he delivered at a Territorial smoking concert in Maidstone, when the idea of there being a war wasn't on any horizon, he predicted that if war came at all it would be with the suddenness of a thief in the night, and must not find the nation unready or unprepared, a warning which, we fear, was simply regarded as the usual post-prandial oratory.

Although newspapers provide the best accounts they can of wartime incidents, with assumptions sometimes being the order of the day, to determine the intricacies of what happened a firsthand account by somebody who was actually there is hard to beat. One such letter was sent by Sergeant G.W. Turner to his fiancée Miss Daisy Gibbons of Burnt Barn Farm, Leeds, near Maidstone. The topic of his writing was the Battle of Mons. Sergeant Turner was wounded during the Battle of Mons and wrote his letter from the Convent Nemy in Belgium where he was being treated:

> *I was wounded about one and a half hours after the battle commenced, and lay in the trenches for nine hours. The bullets and shells were flying all round, and did not cease till after dark. Then was my only chance to get out. I crawled on my hands and knees to a little Inn, and there my wounds were dressed. The officer of my company, who was some distance off, sent a stretcher to carry me away, but I had two wounded men with me who could not stand, so I let one of them have the stretcher, and I managed to walk the distance of one mile.*
>
> *We are in a convent which has been made in to a temporary hospital, and the convent sisters and other Belgian ladies are very kind to us. Two of them are paying particular attention to me. They keep coming and propping*

me up in bed and giving me barley water and cigarettes, and bathe my head with eau de Cologne. The women who are looking after us are very brave. The sight of the wounded when I came here last night was enough to turn trained nurses, but they did their work bravely.

We lost a lot of men yesterday. One company was nearly wiped out. Of two companies of 400 men, only 60 are left. Today shrapnel has been bursting all round, but the hospital was not touched, except for one bullet which struck a window. The bullet that wounded me went in to one breast pocket and came out of the other, and in its course it passed through your photo, making a hole in the breast, as in mine. What a strange coincidence! It passed through my watch and struck a large clasp knife, smashing it to pieces, and driving it through my pocket.

It must have been such a relief for Daisy to receive and read her fiancé's letter, especially as initially he was reported missing. Before the war Sergeant Turner had worked in a school as a gymnastics instructor.

Two of Daisy's brothers also served during the first World War. Horace was in the Royal Navy between July 1916 and April 1918 and was based for some of the time at Chatham. Sydney was a Sapper with the Royal Engineers. He enlisted on 14 April 1916, served in France between 22 July 1916 and 19 July 1917, and was discharged on 5 July 1918 for being no longer physically fit enough for war service. He suffered a gunshot wound to his right arm while fighting in France. Sydney and Daisy's fiancé both recovered from their wounds and survived the war.

On Friday, 25 September 1914, a letter appeared in the *Kent & Sussex Courier* which had been written by Sergeant W. Holmes of the Queen's Own (Royal West Kent Regiment) who at the time was serving with the British Expeditionary Force. It read as follows:

We are off again, this time with some of the French, and it's enough to give you fits to hear the Frenchmen trying to pick up the words of 'Cheer, Boys, Cheer,' which we great 'go' on the march.

They haven't any notion of what the words mean, but they can tell from our manner that they mean we're in good heart, and that's infectious here.

We lost our Colonel and four other officers in our fight on Tuesday. It was the hottest thing we were ever in. The Colonel was struck down when he was giving us the last word of advice before we threw ourselves on the enemy. We avenged him in fine style.

His loss was a great blow to us, for he was very popular. It's always the best officers, somehow, that get hit the first, and there's not a man in the Regiment who wouldn't have given his life for him. He was keen on discipline, but soldiers don't think any less of officers who are that.

The German officers are a rum lot. They don't seem in too great a hurry to expose their precious carcases, and so they 'lead' from the rear all the time.

We see to it that they don't benefit much by that, you may be sure, and when it's at all possible we shoot at the skulking officers. That probably accounts for the high death rate among German officers.

They seem terribly keen on pushing their men forward in to posts of danger, but they are not so keen in leading the way, except in retreat, when they are well to the fore.

Our cavalry are up to that little dodge and so when they are riding out to intercept retreating Germans, they always give special attention to the officers.

What strikes me when reading such letters, written by men from the other ranks, is the humour in their words, even though they are writing about extremely serious matters.

Sergeant Fuller of the Queen's Own (Royal West Kent Regiment) wrote of his experiences during the Battle of Mons and the death of a Lieutenant Anderson:

During the morning of Sunday August 23rd, a party of cavalry was sent forward to carry out reconnaissance. My company, that is 'A' Company, was told to cover their retirement if necessary. We had not got far out of town before we heard firing. The cavalry and some cyclists pushed forward, and, meanwhile we did the best we could to make cover for ourselves.

After waiting a while we saw a party of cyclists come back minus their bicycles. We asked what was wrong, and they told us they had been pursued by Germans. About a quarter of an hour after they passed us the Germans appeared on our front about five hundred yards away. Naturally we opened fire at once, and about the same time shells began to fall around us.

It was not long before Lieut. Anderson, who was lying close to me, received a rifle bullet in the head, it could not have been a shell that killed him or I should have got it as well. Shortly afterwards, however, I was myself hit in the face by a piece of a shell which exploded near by. I then started making my way to the rear, but had hardly left cover when I received a bullet through the thigh. I was taken into hospital, I believe it was really a nunnery, where I had my face stitched and my leg attended to. I should think it was about midnight when a messenger came in and told us that all those who could move had better get away. Most of us got out, and we had to reach the railway station the best we could. Having arrived there, we entrained down to Amiens. I believe we arrived there on the Monday morning. We stayed until the following Friday, when we went to Havre, travelling in a cattle truck.

Lieutenant Anderson, or Colin Knox Anderson, was 26 years of age when he was killed in action on 23 August 1914. He was with the 3rd Battalion but attached to 'A' Company, 1st Battalion, Queen's Own (Royal West Kent Regiment). He is buried at the Military Cemetery in the Belgian village of Hautrage.

At the beginning of October Lady Castlereagh, the wife of the Member of Parliament for Maidstone, Lord Castlereagh, received a letter from him while he was serving in France, in which he told her a little of his experiences. The thing that impressed him the most was the Royal Flying Corps, or what he liked to refer to as the aeroplane service. 'A splendid lot of boys, who really do not know what fear is.' He described how the Germans fired shrapnel at the aircraft in an effort to bring them down and when they exploded they looked like 'little puffs of white smoke', but luckily the shots missed their targets and none of the British aircraft had been brought down.

Lord Castlereagh had been in the Army since 22 May 1895 when he was commissioned as a Second Lieutenant in the 2nd Durham (Seaham) Artillery Volunteer Corps, which later became the 1st Durham Volunteer Artillery. Two years later, after passing out from Sandhurst, he was commissioned into the Royal Horse Guards as a Second Lieutenant. Further promotions followed, but his military career was put on hold when he became the Member of Parliament for Maidstone at the 1906 General Election. He kept his commission and was placed on the half pay list. He was sent out to France in the early weeks of the war as Captain Castlereagh MP, as he was still representing Maidstone in the Houses of Parliament. His role was that of ADC to General William Pulteney, whose headquarters were in Paris, where he arrived on 29 August 1914. Despite his position he saw action within a matter of days of his arrival, exposing him to the true horrors of war and the pain and suffering of wounded British soldiers. On 7 November he was promoted to the rank of Major. He was to have quite a busy and varied wartime experience, but here I will look only at the period leading up to October 1914. His career will be looked at in more depth in the chapter on 'Maidstone's Famous' later in this book.

Colonel F.S.W. Cornwallis received a commission with the Reserve Regiment of the West Kent Yeomanry in early October 1914 and in doing so he relinquished his position as the Commanding Officer of the 1st Kent (Maidstone Battalion) National Reserve. He wrote a letter to the officers and men who he left behind:

I cannot leave without a word of farewell and expression of my gratitude to the officers, section leaders and men for their loyal support. It is impossible to give an accurate figure of the number of those who have joined the Regular or Territorial Forces from this Battalion since war was declared, but I know the number to be very considerable, and I feel, therefore that while we have maintained and cemented old comradeships, we have at the same time been able to render service to our King and country.

A meeting took place in Maidstone on Tuesday, 13 October 1914, at a smoking concert in connection with the West Kent Yeomanry. Those in attendance included the Mayor of Maidstone, Viscount Hythe, and the Marquis Camden. It was the Viscount who first addressed the meeting. He said that long before the war and at a time when he was still in command of the Regiment, he recognized the need to form a Yeomanry Reserve. When the war broke out he started to collate a list of men, including his own, who had previously served with and who were willing to rejoin the Yeomanry.

By October 1914 they had been back together for nearly a month and he was proud to be back in command of such a loyal and committed group of men. Their training had been helped by the cooperation of Lord Camden and the fact that he had been able to secure the services of past officers of the Regiment, such as Colonel Cornwallis, who had from a sense of duty to his country in a time of need, accepted a position of squadron leader, a man under whom Lord Hythe had previously served. Major Mills had also rejoined. This was the man who to his credit had led the West Kent Yeomanry throughout the South African War which lasted for two and a half years between 11 October 1899 and 31 May 1902. Major Davison, who had previously been the Yeomanry's Quartermaster, had also rejoined.

Lord Hythe was happy in the knowledge that if every officer and man of the Yeomanry trained hard and gave of their best, they would become an efficient and durable regiment and serve both Maidstone and their country well. He gave a toast to those who were in attendance at the meeting and to the health of the town's Mayor who had previously been a trooper in the regiment. Although a Territorial unit, the men who joined the West Kent Yeomanry were not obliged to serve overseas. Despite this all but six of them volunteered to do so, and these had good reasons for not doing so, which Lord Hythe openly supported, although he believed that if asked by the War Office to serve overseas, that all of the regiment would willingly do so.

The First World War affected people in many different ways and it sometimes made them look at others they had known for many years in a totally different light, especially when fear and uncertainty became part of the equation. One aspect of this was rumour control. A comment with absolutely no foundation to it at all other than an individual's incorrect belief could become a fact in no time at all. This issue resulted in Harry J. Sancto of Clare House in Ticehurst writing a letter to the editor of the *Kent & Sussex Courier* which appeared in the edition dated 23 October 1914:

> *Sir,*
>
> *May I, through the medium of your valuable paper, contradict the rumour that is going round the Ticehurst district that I am a German. I am not even naturalized, but a real Englishman, being born in Maidstone, Kent, and my parents and grandparents were Kentish people.*
>
> *It is interesting to note in the Sussex archaeological Collections Vol. VXII, that Sir Robert De Sancto Leodegario came to England with William the Conqueror in 1066, so probably my origin is more English than some of those who pass remarks.*

This wouldn't be the only occasion when passion and national fervour got the better of people, and sometimes it resulted in violence or damage to innocent people and their property.

In the same edition of the newspaper there was an article about the West Kent Quarter Sessions which took place at the Sessions House in Maidstone on Thursday, 22 October 1914. One of the cases heard that day concerned a young man by the name of Emmanuel Ert who was 23 years of age and a labourer. He was charged with stealing a pearl diamond platinum pendant and chain, 12 silver forks, 5 silver spoons, 6 fish knives, and one fish slice and fork, all belonging to Eliza Colquhoun Redhouse. Ert was further charged with stealing a silver watch, a gold chain and a cigarette case, that all belonged to Colonel George Phillips. He pleaded guilty to both charges, and also guilty to a previous conviction against him from a case which took place at the Central Criminal Court in 1912 where he was convicted of having committed similar offences. The defendant, Ert, had taken a position with Colonel Phillips at his house on 1 August, leaving the very next day having stolen the abovementioned items. He was subsequently arrested in London where he was found to be in possession of a number of pawn tickets which related to the items that Ert had stolen. The estimated value of the items was twenty pounds. The police officer in the case, Detective Hadlow, outlined Ert's previous convictions dating back to 1906 which included a sentence of three years' penal servitude in 1912. There had been an occasion in Southend-on-Sea when he was employed at the Royal Hotel but dismissed for dishonesty, but the manager decided not to report the matter to the police. Two nights later while still in the area he broke into a home in Westcliffe Parade and stole a quantity of jewellery and some cash. The chairman of the bench sentenced Ert to a period of five years' penal servitude. Detective Hadlow then informed the court that the prisoner's parents were both German, that his father had been deported in January earlier that year, and there was no doubting that Ert had German origins. Ert told the court that he was not German, he was English, having been born in the City of London and that Detective Hadlow had a personal vendetta against him. Ert's remonstrations were to no avail and the chairman of the bench informed him that once he had served his sentence he faced deportation to Germany.

Other offences heard at the Quarterly Sessions included an assault in which a woman had stabbed a man in the eye with a hat pin, an indecent assault, motoring offences and theft.

Even though there was a war going on, the cases heard before the Quarterly Sessions on that day showed that normal life still went ahead regardless and that the law was still strictly enforced.

The Kent & Sussex Courier dated 30 October 1914 included an article about the 4th Battalion, Queen's Own (Royal West Kent Regiment), which was a Territorial unit that had been raised for home service and was stationed at Maidstone. The regiment's officer in command was Lieutenant Colonel Simpson, with his deputy being Major Cohen. The battalion's headquarters while they were stationed in Maidstone, and where both officers and men were billeted, was the Corn Exchange. During the week, the men of the battalion undertook route marches with drummers and trumpeters at their front.

On Thursday, 29 October, the entire battalion attended the funeral of one of its own. Private Fryer, who was one of the men who had volunteered for overseas service, was wounded and invalided home. Private 2271 T. Fryer was a married man and died at the Depot Hospital of the 3rd Battalion, Queen's Own (Royal West Kent Regiment) on Monday, 26 October 1914. He was 33 years of age and is buried at Maidstone Cemetery.

On 31 October 1914 the Baroness Orczy, who was a famous novelist of the time, attended the Maidstone Girls' Grammar School to present prizes and deliver a speech. She said that after the war nothing in the world would be quite the same as before. 'For one thing,' she said, 'the era of the half educated, half baked, half trained woman would be at an end.' She saw the new world that would rise like a phoenix out of the ashes of the war as one that would belong to the efficient alone and she emphasized that she felt women could be a part of that new world, regardless of the path they chose, whether professional, commercial, nursing or even scrubbing floors. As long as they did it with absolute thoroughness and efficiency, then they would be successful in their endeavours. Baroness Orczy, or, to give her her full title, Baroness Emma Magdolna Rozália Mária Jozefa Borbála Orczy de Orci, was born in Hungary in 1865 and moved to London in 1880 where she became a novelist, playwright and artist. She is best known for her novels featuring the Scarlet Pimpernel.

By November 1914 the number of wounded soldiers being sent back to the UK from the Western Front and from other theatres of war was much greater than had ever been anticipated by the military authorities. At the beginning of November thirty-five wounded British soldiers, who had originally been patients at Fort Pitt Military Hospital in Chatham, had recovered enough to be moved. They were sent to two locations in the Maidstone District. Nineteen of them were sent to the Workhouse at Hollingbourne which is situated some four miles to the east of the centre of Maidstone. Remarkably, these nineteen men came from eighteen different regiments from all different parts of the UK. Hollingbourne was quite possibly the first workhouse to accommodate wounded British soldiers. Part of the workhouse had been used as a hospital for infectious diseases dating back to 1886. The remaining sixteen men were placed under the care of the staff of the VAD Hospital at Hayle Place. Nearly all of them were sent home after being wounded at Armentières, most of them with gunshot wounds to their hands and legs.

On 24 November 1914 Mr Justice Lawrence arrived in Maidstone in preparation for the Kent Assizes. On his arrival, not only did he find the High Sheriff of Kent wasn't waiting for him as was customary, but his usual lodgings were unavailable as well. But he wasn't angry; in the circumstances, he completely understood. The High Sheriff, Mr Francis Elmer Speed, was absent, away on active service, and the usual lodgings put at the disposal of the Judge attending the Assizes had been commandeered for billeting the officers of the West Kent Yeomanry. Instead Mr Justice Lawrence was a guest of the acting High Sheriff, Sir Mark Collet, who lived at the Mote, Maidstone.

Besides being the High Sheriff of Kent, Sir Mark was also the Squire of Knowlton, living at Knowlton Court, and a major in the Royal East Kent Yeomanry. At the outbreak of the war he was already 55 years old. His two sons also served during the war, Captain John Speed, who was with the 2nd Life Guards and a holder of the Military Cross, and Captain Douglas Speed, who was with the 60th Rifles. All three men survived the war.

The monthly meeting of the Kent executive of the National Farmers Union took place on Thursday, 3 December 1914, at the Bull Hotel in Maidstone. During wartime an effective farming industry was essential for the country's welfare as well as making it less reliant on imports from abroad. The main topics of discussion on a cold and overcast day in Maidstone that day were the Navy's appeal for fresh fruit and vegetables, shortage of labour to collect the crops, sugar beet and the possibility of a factory, and hop growing and beer duty. A letter was read out from Lord Charles Beresford on behalf of the Vegetable Products Committee appealing to farmers to form districtwide committees with a view to sending fresh fruit, vegetables and preserved fruits to sailors serving on board the nation's warships.

Lord Charles Beresford.

The chairman of the meeting, Mr Champion, confirmed that such schemes were in place in other areas because they were actively supported by similar associations as their own. He commended the idea and supported those who cared to follow suit. Lord Beresford had a vested interest in writing his letter. He had a long and illustrious connection with the British Royal Navy, having served in it for an amazing fifty-two years, between 1859 and 1911, ending up with the rank of admiral. His brother William had won a Victoria Cross during the Anglo-Zulu War of 1879, the war made famous by the Battle of Rorke's Drift.

A continued lack of labour in the farming industry was a growing concern due in the main to the number of men who were enlisting in the army, many of whom had previously worked as farm labourers. It was foreseen that the longer the war continued the worse this situation was going to get. A resolution was put forward by the Cranbrook Farmers Association that owing to the shortage of farm labour due to the war, Kent Education Committee should allow children who had reached their 12th birthday to be employed for agricultural purposes for the remainder of the war. Although those at the meeting understood that it would not be as straightforward a proposition as it looked on the surface, a letter would be forwarded to the Kent Education Committee in an attempt at progressing the matter.

Sugar shortages were the cause of many a wartime conversation, including at this meeting. It was stated that a large amount of financial capital would be needed to be able to build a sugar factory, and for that to be achieved, ten or twelve of the country's beet growers would be needed to commit to it to make it work. A decision on the matter was put off so that it could be discussed further at the Union's next Annual General Meeting.

A discussion on hop growing and beer duty took up most of the meeting, a matter about which there was a great deal of concern. The main issue was on the government's intention to raise the duty on beer and how this would affect barley and hop growers. In 1914 the British public were consuming 36 million barrels of beer a year and the government's intention was to increase the duty on it by four shillings a barrel, which was not only a massive increase for the wholesalers, but for the ordinary man every time he drank a pint of beer. Although the National Farmers Union accepted the government's reasons for the rise, they wanted it to be a graduated one rather than a large increase in one go. There was also the suggestion from the meeting that the government should look to place a duty charge on imported foreign hops, rather than penalize British workers. A duty increase at the level which the government wanted to impose it had far reaching implications for the industry, including potential for ruin for brewers and the possibility that the government would have to step in to save them. The Union's argument was if an increase in the duty on beer was likely to result in such an outcome, why impose it, as it would ultimately end up back in the lap of government to unravel.

On Wednesday, 9 December 1914, Mr A.P. Hedges was speaking at a recruitment meeting for regular soldiers of His Majesty's armed forces on the subject of the formation of a local Volunteer Training Corps, held at Maidstone Town Hall. He mentioned how it struck him that in relation to the Volunteer Training Corps movement, there were a number of men, who by reason of age or other infirmities, were incapable of serving in either the Regular Army or the Territorial Force, but who were still keen to do their bit to help their country in its time of need. Mr Hedges wanted to push the idea of a local Volunteer Training Corps and warned of the danger of a German invasion of Great Britain. He saw the war as being a long road and that if a Volunteer Training Corps was formed and properly trained they could effectively undertake the role of home defence which in turn would release soldiers to go and fight the Germans across the Channel and hopefully prevent them from then being able to invade Great Britain. Mr Hedges ended his speech with the following words:

> It was a matter for the man to decide for himself his position, and when the war was a matter of history, and they were telling the story of the troubled times, it would be a poor excuse for them to tell the inquiring boys and girls: I did not go because there was a fellow who lived next door to me who did not go. Is that an answer? It won't be an answer then, and it is no answer today. Let every man's heart echo the words of the Prophet of old, 'Here I am, send me.'

Others who addressed the meeting were Sir Reginald Maclead and Mr K. McAlpine. It was a unanimous decision to form a Maidstone and District Volunteer Training Corps.

Christmas day on the Western Front was one of rejoicing, as men on both sides stopped fighting, put down their weapons and even played football against each other in no man's land, as humanity briefly returned to the world.

Meanwhile back home in Britain the people of Kent received a slightly different type of goodwill message, in the form of an official letter from the Vice-Lieutenant of Kent, Lord Harris, sent on behalf of the Lord Lieutenant, the Marquis Camden, who was out of the county on active service. The letter was a list of instructions as to what the civilian population should do in the event of an invasion by German forces. The Marquis began his letter by pointing out that in order to be recognized officially as a combatant, a volunteer must be a member of a Volunteer Training Corps that was affiliated to the Central Association of Volunteer Training Corps, and that only members of such Corps would receive the badge that was issued by government. Any civilian who was not in possession of the official Government badge could not be counted as a combatant and had to surrender any firearms which they had in their possession. There was an important reason for this: in the event of an invasion, anybody engaged in armed resistance against the Germans who did not possess a government badge was liable to be shot if caught. The letter was somewhat contradictory as it went in to great detail about what local civilian populations should do in the event of an invasion, but then went out of its way to point out that all and any of the measures that had been advised were only precautionary and that the chances of any hostile landings on the shores of the United Kingdom were no more likely to occur in December 1914 than they had been in the early days and weeks of the war. The letter pointed out that the better prepared the civilian population was to assist regular army units in repelling any hostile invasion, the more chance there was of such a defence being a successful one.

If a town wished to form its own Voluntary Training Corps, it first had to contact the Central Association of Voluntary Training Corps that was located at the Royal Courts of Justice in London for further information.

Within a week of the meeting, members of the Maidstone and District Voluntary Training Corps had commenced their first training course for recruits. Amongst those present at the first drill was the

Deputy-Mayor, Councillor A.T. Ebbs, previously of the West Kent Yeomanry. Also present was Councillor S. Dyke as well as many other prominent and professional gentlemen of the town.

Kent, like every other county throughout Britain, had its own Emergency Committee which would liaise with the county constabulary and the relevant military authority in the event of an invasion to deter and challenge the enemy as effectively as possible.

Lessons had been learnt from the naval bombardments of Hartlepool, Whitby and Scarborough only a week earlier, where residents took to the streets to see what was going on. This was partly responsible for the high casualty numbers; 137 people were killed in the attack and another 592 were injured. The advice to the people of Maidstone was to seek shelter underground.

CHAPTER 3

1915
Deepening Conflict

The war moved in to its second year with no sign of it coming to an end any time soon.

The Battle of Loos, which took place over three days between 25 and 28 September, had been preceded by a four-day artillery bombardment in which a staggering quarter of a million shells had been fired.

In charge of the attack was Douglas Haig who, despite the fact that the British and French forces outnumbered German forces in some places by seven to one, had misgivings about the overall plan. He wasn't happy about the terrain that his men would have to cross to get to their objectives, and that his men were not in their best physical state, having already been involved in numerous battles earlier in the year. These included the Battle of Neuve Chapelle in March, the 2nd Battle of Ypres in April, the Battle of Hill 60 in April, and the 2nd Battle of Artois in May and June.

The Battle of Loos was the first time that the British Army had used poison gas against the Germans. In total they released 5,100 cylinders of chlorine, about 140 tons in total. The plan was not a success as in some places the strong winds blew the gas back towards the British trenches, resulting in 2,632 casualties, seven of whom died. By the end of the battle, which lasted for thirteen days, British forces had suffered nearly 50,000 casualties, of whom more than 20,000 were killed. British casualties were estimated to be twice as high as German. A total of twenty-one Victoria Crosses were awarded to British troops for their acts of bravery, two posthumously.

Throughout 1915, 151,774 British and Commonwealth servicemen were killed. This included 1,470 members of The Buffs (East Kent Regiment) and 870 members of the Queen's Own (Royal West Kent Regiment), many of whom were from Maidstone (this is not of course to suggest that these are the only two regiments that men from Maidstone served with). This was the backdrop to which Maidstone carried on her everyday existence.

The Reserve Regiment of the West Kent (Queen's Own) Yeomanry moved from their barracks in Maidstone to their new home at the Cavalry Barracks at Hounslow in January 1915. The Regiment's 1/1st Battalion, which included 'D' Squadron, stationed at Maidstone, were mobilized on the first day of the war. They remained in England, mainly in the Canterbury area, until 24 September 1915 when they sailed from Liverpool on board the RMS *Olympic* which before the war had been a transatlantic passenger liner of the White Star Line but for the duration of the war operated as a troopship. They arrived at the Greek Island of Lemnos on 1 October 1915 and at Gallipoli a week later on 8 October.

Between 7 November 1915 and 27 December 1915, ten members of the regiment were killed or died of their wounds during the fighting at Gallipoli. They were:

Private 812 Henry A. Davies.
Private 1421 George B. Atkins.
Private 1839 Walter J. Boorer.
Private 743 Ernest George Glass.
Private 1014 R. Holmes.
Private 1949 Francis Geoffrey Everard James.
Private 996 William John Bates.
Private 1067 Reginald Gordon McMurray.
Private 1709 James Arthur Beal.
Private 734 Cecil Charles Theobald.

They were either buried at the Twelve Tree Copse or Pink Farm cemeteries in Helles, or their names are commemorated on the Helles Memorial. Another member of the regiment, Private 801 Cyril Adlington Boorman from Gravesend, died six months before the regiment left to go to war, on 3 March 1915, and is buried at the Gravesend Cemetery in Kent. He was 23 years of age and was born and bred in Gravesend with the family home being Maycroft, 143 Wrotham Road. Cyril's case is an interesting one. According to the *De Ruvigny's Roll of Honour, 1914-1919*, he was posthumously promoted to the rank of lieutenant, which at first glance doesn't make an awful lot of sense. He had joined the West Kent Yeomanry in 1913 and on the outbreak of the war, when his regiment was mobilized, he volunteered for foreign service. While undergoing training at Westbere near Canterbury he contracted cerebro-spinal meningitis and died on 3 March 1915. He was gazetted as a 2nd Lieutenant with the Royal Engineers on 27 March 1915, the date of his commission coming into effect on 1 March 1915, two days before he passed away. This is possibly one of the few cases of a man being gazetted for a commission after he had died. On his death, a friend and colleague, Lieutenant the Hon. A.R. Mills, wrote:

> *He joined the troop with me in 1913, and was near me for two trainings and of course, since mobilization, and was one of my most efficient men, intelligent, keen and a first rate soldier, and I feel sure would have made an excellent officer.*

Boorman was in his school cricket eleven for several years as well as being captain of the football team. He also held the school's long jump record.

The case of Cecil Charles Theobald shows how research can throw up ambiguities. The Commonwealth War Graves Commission website and the Graves Registration Report for Twelve Trees Copse Cemetery both show his date of death as 8 December 1915. But the Army Register of Soldiers' Effects shows that he was killed in action on 18 December 1915, and the Medal Rolls Index for First World War soldiers shows that he was discharged from the Army on 1 September 1917.

By the end of the war a further twenty-five members of the West Kent (Queen's Own) Yeomanry had fallen victim to the war. In no particular order they were:

Private 2515 J.S. Turner
Private 2059 L.C.E. Thomas
Private 2093 Albert Edward Luck
Private 1539 H. Mann
Private 2347 Maurice Chapman
Private 2131 John Richard Fagg
Private 245375 Bertie Alfred Baker
Private 245365 F.E. Chick
Private 245330 J. Leary
Private 2468 F.L. Smith
Private 2448 O.F. Maier
Private 245321 H. Taylor
Private 2204 Charles Gilbert
Private 245399 Arthur Edmund Fermor
Private 2331 Albert Ellis
Private 24514 Geoffrey Frank Dowling
Private 2521 Thomas Darby
Private 245346 Arthur J Coulter
Private 2304 Thomas William Hopkins
Private 2374 Harry Gordon Nicholls
Private 2096 Harry Noakes
Private 2215 Herbert James Taunt
Private 245351 Sidney Charles Ingram
Private 245368 Alfred Henry Jopson
Private 245369 William Victor Long

A total of eighteen of these men were killed on the same day, 31 August 1916, during the Battle of the Somme. Of these thirteen have no known grave as their bodies were never found, but their names are commemorated on the Thiepval Memorial.

It has to be remembered that many other men also served with the regiment, but then transferred on to and served with other units, some of whom paid the ultimate price.

An article appeared in the *Kent & Sussex Courier* on Friday, 8 January 1915. It was about the prospective Conservative candidate for Maidstone, Carlyon Bellairs, who had been a commander in the Royal Navy, in which he had served from 1895 to 1902. He had also previously been the Liberal Member of Parliament for King's Lynn and he wrote for the *Evening Standard* newspaper on Naval affairs. He founded the Parliamentary Navy Committee in line with his disagreement of British Naval policy, which did not negatively affect his naval career, which was a very distinguished one, and included the position of lecturer for the War Course to Senior Naval officers at the Royal Naval College between 1902 and 1903.

Carlyon Bellairs became the MP for Maidstone as a result of the by-election on 22 February 1915 which came about as the result of the succession of the incumbent MP, Charles Vane-Tempest-Stewart, as the 7th Marquess of Londonderry. Because of an agreed wartime political pact for one party not to challenge the other, Carlyon Bellairs was elected unopposed. He was also re-elected to the Maidstone seat in the 1918 General Election. His time in Maidstone was spent living with his wife Charlotte at Gore Court.

Carlyon Bellairs.

There were other events which took place during 1915 which, although happening far from Maidstone, are still worthy of mention as indirectly they would have still had an effect on the town.

This was the year which saw the first Zeppelin raid take place over Britain. On the evening of 19/20 January 1915, two Zeppelins dropped bombs in and around the Great Yarmouth area of Norfolk. The raid had initially been intended for the Humberside area, but strong winds determined that the German raiders had to choose another target. Four people were killed in the raid, as well as damage caused to a number of properties. In that one evening, the war suddenly became very real, as it came straight to the front door of the British people.

British and Allied troops landed in Gallipoli on 25 April 1915 and didn't leave until 9 January 1916. During those eight months, two weeks and one day, the British and their Allies incurred an estimated 252,000 casualties. The Ottoman Empire suffered a similar number.

The sinking of the Cunard ocean going liner RMS *Lusitania* took place on Friday, 7 May 1915, when the German submarine *U-20* torpedoed her in the North Atlantic near Kinsale, Ireland. Out of 1,959 passengers and crew, 1,198 of them perished. The incident was believed to be largely responsible for America's entry into the First World War.

Andrew Bratley, an amateur historian originally from Maidstone but who now lives with his family in Perth, Western Australia, carried out research into men from Kent who served with the Australian Army during the First World War. After visiting over fifty war memorials in Western Australia, he discovered that 223 of the men mentioned on them had been born in Kent. Of these, a number originated from Maidstone.

John Bowles was 35 years of age and a private, 6707, in the Australian Imperial Force when he died of his wounds on 14 September 1918. He is buried at the Heath Cemetery, Harbonnières in the Somme region of France. Although he lived in the Mount Barker district, his parents lived at Martins Farm, Boughton, Monchelsea, Maidstone.

William Craddock was 38 years of age and a petty officer stoker, 1825, serving in the Royal Australian Navy on board HMAS *Barambah* when he died of pneumonia on 17 October 1918. His name is commemorated on the Plymouth Naval Memorial. His parents, William and Sarah Craddock, lived at Tovil in Maidstone, although his home in Australia was at 51 Dove Road, North Williamstown, Victoria.

Henry Hodgson was 40 years of age and a sergeant (906) in the 17th Battalion, Australian Imperial Force, when he died of his wounds on 9 August 1918. He is buried at the Villers Bretonneux Military Cemetery in the Somme region. His home in Australia was 3 Woollcot Street, Darlinghurst, New South Wales, but he was born in Maidstone in 1878.

Female survivor from the Lusitania.

Group photo of Australian soldiers.

George Hodgkin was 27 years of age and an able seaman (RN/226508) with the Royal Navy but attached to the Royal Australian Navy. Although every death in wartime is sad, Able Seaman Hodgkin's death was particularly poignant. Along with twenty of his colleagues he had been loaned to the Royal Australian Navy for just three days. During this time Able Seaman Hodgkin served on the submarine HMAS *AE1.* At seven o'clock in the morning on 14 September 1914, *AE1*, along with HMAS *Parramatta,* left from Blanche Bay in Rabul, Papua New Guinea, to patrol in the area of Cape Gazelle. She was never seen or heard of again in spite of a search by several other vessels who were sent to look for her. No wreckage or bodies of any of the thirty-five crew have ever been found. There is no belief that she was sunk by a German U-Boat; it is more probable that she sank after striking some kind of underwater obstacle.

The loss of HMAS *AE1* along with all of her crew was hard enough for the families to contend with, but to not know where their final resting place was, and how they died, must have been all the more painful.

Australian submarine 'AE1'.

Jabez Kingsley was 46 years of age and a private (976) in the 32nd Battalion, Australian Imperial Army, when he died of his wounds on 25 June 1918. He is buried at the Vignacourt British Cemetery, which is situated in the Somme region of France. He was born in Maidstone, but lived in Perth, Western Australia.

Leslie Gordon Norley was 24 years of age and a sergeant (20030) in the 8th Brigade, Australian Field Artillery, when he was killed in action at Menin Road on 14 September 1917. He is buried at the Huts Cemetery in the West-Vlaanderen (West Flanders) region of Belgium. Nearly two-thirds of the 1,094 British and Allied men who are buried there from the First World War were gunners from the numerous artillery units which were positioned in the area. His home was in Woodanilling, Western Australia, but his parents, William and Eliza Norley, lived at 75 Salisbury Road, Maidstone.

The Honourable Leopold Florence Scarlett was 25 years of age, born in Hampshire on 17 March 1889 and a lieutenant in the Royal Navy. Like George Hodgkin, he was attached to the Royal Australian Navy and was also one of the crew members of the Australian submarine HMAS *AE1* when she was lost on 14 September 1914. His name is commemorated on the Plymouth Naval Memorial. His mother, Mrs Bessie Florence Scarlett, lived at Penenden House, Maidstone. His father, Lieutenant Colonel Leopold James Scarlett of the Royal Scots Guards, had been born in Florence, Italy, hence Leopold's middle name. His brother Lawrence James Peter Scarlett was also a Navy man and died on 22 June 1893 while serving onboard HMS *Victory*. Another of his brothers, Commander Shelley Leopold Laurence Scarlett, Royal Naval Volunteer Reserve, died on 23 May 1917 aged 45. He was also the 5th Baron Abinger. Robert Brooke Campbell Scarlett was a Navy man and survived the war. He was the 6th Baron Abinger. Lieutenant Colonel Hugh Richard Scarlett, the 7th Baron Abinger, was commissioned as a second lieutenant in the Royal Artillery on 26 May 1900 and fought in both the Second Boer War (1900-2) and the First World War, earning himself the Distinguished Service Order. Major General Percy Gerald Scarlett was mentioned in despatches and was a holder of the Military Cross. He served through the First World War and from 1939 to 1942 in the Second World War.

William Henry Watt was 44 years of age and a private (3210) in the 24th Battalion, Australian Imperial Force, when he was killed in action on 9 October 1917. He lived at 2 Campbell Street, Coburg, Victoria, Australia. He has no known grave and his name is commemorated on the Menin Gate Memorial. He was born in Maidstone.

Richard Charles Wynn was 29 years of age and was a private (7087) in the 16th Battalion, Australian Infantry Force, when he died of his wounds on 27 September 1917. He is buried at the Huts Cemetery, which is situated in the West-Vlaanderen region of Belgium. His mother, Charlotte Wynn, lived at 10 Heath Grove, Barming Heath, Maidstone. Before moving to Perth in Western Australia, Richard was a nurseryman at the Bunyard Nursery in Maidstone.

Thomas Edward Dines was a private (1115) in the 11th Battalion, Australian Imperial Force, and was born at Broughton Malherbe, near Maidstone. His father, William Dines, lived at Lower Shipway, Willington, Maidstone.

He had enlisted at a town called Blackboy Hill in Western Australia on 31 October 1914 and died of wounds received fighting at Mustapha in Egypt on 15 May 1915.

Cecil Vernon Down was 22 years of age and a private (805) in the 16th Battalion, Australian

Thomas Edward Dines.

Imperial Force, when he was killed in action at Gallipoli. His name is commemorated on the Lone Pine Memorial in Turkey. He had enlisted at Helena Vale in Western Australia on 25 September 1914.

Cecil was born in Maidstone and his mother Lizzie still lived in the town at 38 Hedley Street. Before the war he had worked in a Bank.

Albert Henry Hooker was 28 years of age and a private (3063) in the 13th Battalion, Australian Imperial Force. He had enlisted in Australia on 4 August 1915 and had left for France a month later on 6 September 1915 on board HMAT *Ballarat*. He was killed in action on 29 August 1916 and buried at the Australian Imperial Force Burial Grounds at Flers in the Somme region of France. Before the war he had been an engine driver and a flour mill labourer. His father, Horace Hooker, lived at Adamswell Farm, West Peckham, Maidstone.

Cecil Vernon Down.

William Beal enlisted in Sydney, New South Wales, just two weeks after the start of the war on 19 August 1914 and became a private (898) in the 3rd Battalion, Australian Imperial Force. On 21 May 1915, he had been wounded in action during fighting at Gallipoli when he received gunshot wounds to his right arm. He was 27 years of age when he was killed in action on 6 August 1915. His name is commemorated on the Lone Pine Memorial in Turkey. His mother, Mrs F.J. Beal, lived at Todwell Farm, Offham, near Maidstone.

Harry Ernest Thurston was already 35 years of age when he enlisted in the Australian Imperial Force on 20 August 1914 in Melbourne, Victoria, where he lived at 304 Spencer Street. He became a private (609) in the 6th Battalion. He was killed in action at Gallipoli on 25 April 1915 and his name is commemorated on the Lone Pine Memorial in Turkey. His sister Esther lived at 54 Dover Street, Maidstone.

Cyril Frederick Larking enlisted on 31 October 1914 in Liverpool, New South Wales, and became a private (609) in the 6th Battalion, Australian Imperial Force. He died of his wounds, a gunshot to his stomach, while on board HMHS *Dunluce Castle* on his way back to

England on 10 August 1915. He was 23 years of age.

He was born at West Malling on the outskirts of Maidstone and on emigrating to Australia moved to Millers Point in New South Wales.

Cyril Frederick Larking.

On Saturday, 9 January 1915, a Maidstone man by the name of Henry Alexander Christy, aged 35, a clerk by profession, who had previously used the alias of G.F. Grevatt, was charged by the police with attempting to obtain charitable donations from the Hon. Rupert Guiness MP by false pretences. He appeared before the Marlborough Street Police Court, London. Detective Sergeant Hedges told the court that he collected Christy from Maidstone Borough Police Station earlier that same day. From there he conveyed him to Vine Street Police station where he read the Warrant to him, the defendant replied, 'I am the man referred to. I have been a fool. I will give you no trouble. I did write the letter from 94 Princes Street, Southend, and I wrote there asking for my letters to be forwarded on to 35 Sandling Road, Maidstone. There is no Victoria Rifle Club. I thought by doing this I should get some money to get me over my trouble, which you know all about. I will plead guilty, and wish to be dealt with straight away for the sake of my children.' Detective Sergeant Hedges also informed the court that Christy had been in trouble for obtaining money from Sir Edward Coates MP and that he had two previous convictions. Christy had got himself into financial difficulties due to keeping two homes while only earning £2 a week in wages and trying to provide for a total of nine children. Despite his honesty and admissions to the offences he was sentenced to three months in prison with hard labour. The 1911 census shows Christy living at 77 Colchester Road, Southend-on-Sea, Essex, and working as an accountant's clerk. He was married to Nellie and at that time they had three children: two daughters, Violet and Edith, and a son, Leslie, who were all under three years of age.

The *Kent & Sussex Courier* of 15 January 1915 included the news that Lieutenant Frederick William Balston, the son of Mr Richard J. Balston of Springfield, Maidstone, and Bilsington Priory, near Ashford, had been appointed to the rank of captain in the Kent Brigade Company, Home Counties Transport section of the Army Service Corps. Frederick survived the war and died at the West Kent General Hospital in Maidstone on 10 January 1965 aged 84.

Mr Balston, who had made his fortune as a manufacturer of paper, had, according to the article, two other sons who also served during the First World War, one of whom, Major George Richard Balston, having served in India, briefly returned to England before going to France with the Royal Horse Artillery. He ended the war at the rank of acting lieutenant colonel and with the award of the Distinguished Service Order. He survived the war and lived to the ripe old age of 88 before passing away in June 1967 in St. Neots, Huntingdonshire.

I found one other son, Richard Arthur E. Balston, but he died in May 1901 at just 14 years of age.

Mr Richard Balston died the following year on 7 December 1916 at 'Springfield' in Maidstone. In his will he left his entire fortune of £144,237 13s 1d (equivalent to over £13 million today) to his daughter Emily.

In the same edition of the newspaper was the sad news of the death of a Maidstone man, George Bertram Pollock-Hodsoll, who had attended the Maidstone Grammar School during the late 1880s before going on to study at University College, Oxford. His actual surname was Hodsoll, with Pollock being one of his middle names. It would appear that the newspaper inadvertently put the two together making his surname appear as Pollock-Hodsoll. George's mother, Georgina was the granddaughter of Sir David Pollock, the Chief Justice of Bombay. She was also the grand-niece of Field Marshal Sir George Pollock, he of Khyber Pass celebrity. This explains where the name Pollock came from. His military career had begun back in December 1902 when he received a commission as a 2nd lieutenant in the Cambridgeshire Militia which was at the time the 4th Battalion, Suffolk Regiment. He subsequently transferred to the 3rd Battalion, Suffolk Regiment, but he was attached to the 1st Battalion, Cheshire Regiment, at the time of his death when he was killed in action leading his men in a counter-attack against German forces during the First Battle of Ypres on 9 November 1914 aged 33, having landed in France two weeks earlier on 23 October 1914. He had also previously been attached to the 1st Battalion, Bedfordshire Regiment. The adjutant, Captain L. Frost, wrote of George to his widow:

> *On 7 Nov. about three o'clock in the afternoon, the reg. on our left fell back and the Germans came through their trenches, so Captain Hodsoll, Mr Anderson and myself with the support of our regt. made a counter attack. Your husband had not gone more than 100 yards when he, poor fellow, was killed. He died instantaneously and could not have suffered any pain at all. He died giving his life for his country at a very critical moment, if this counter attack had failed it would have meant the whole line coming back.*
>
> *He died a glorious and magnificent death. Captain Pollock Hodsoll was buried the same evening on the ground where he died, in a wood near a chateau about three and a half miles east of Ypres. A wooden cross with his name was placed on the grave.*

A thoughtful and nicely worded letter, which may well have skated over the grim way in which he actually died. Personally, I have always struggled with the phrase, 'He died a glorious and magnificent death'. When George's wartime service medals were issued, they were sent to his widow who by then had remarried and was now Mrs Clive Steen, living at the Farm House, Capel, Surrey. George was noted for his sporting prowess, especially football, where he excelled, representing both the Corinthians and Casuals, as well as the Army. He was also heavily involved in the formation of the Amateur Football Association. He has no known grave and his name is commemorated on the Ypres (Menin Gate) Memorial. In his earlier years he had lived with his parents Charles and Georgina Hodsoll at Loose near Maidstone.

On Friday 5 February 1915 the court martial took place at

Maidstone Barracks of Sergeant-Cook Joseph Smith who at the time was serving with the Queen's Own (Royal West Kent Regiment). He was found guilty of stealing a leg of mutton at Maidstone Barracks and reduced to the ranks as well as being sentenced to fifty-six days' imprisonment. The unnamed general who was the commanding officer for the Maidstone district showed some leniency and remitted two weeks of the sentence, meaning that Smith only had to serve forty-two days.

In early February 1915 an interesting article appeared in numerous newspapers up and down the country about the parliamentary seat for Maidstone which had become vacant due to Lord Castlereagh (Charles Vane-Tempest-Stewart, 7th Marquess of Londonderry) having informed his local Conservative executive that he would not seek re-election at the end of the Parliament. This was due to the death of his father, the 6th Marquess. At the time of his father's death, Lord Castlereagh was a captain in the Royal Horse Guards and serving in France. The position was filled by Commander Carlyon Bellairs who was returned unopposed due to a wartime agreement between the different political parties.

What made the article interesting was what it said about Commander Bellairs, who had previously served in the Royal Navy but who had been placed on the retired list in March 1902. He had first been elected to Parliament when he won the seat for the King's Lynn constituency in the 1906 general election for the Liberal party. In February 1915, the *Boston Transcript* newspaper in America reported a conversation between Bellairs and some friends in Montreal in September 1910:

> He [Bellairs] *had no fear of a German outbreak in that year* [1910], *since, so far as he could see, the German programme of Army and Navy expansion would not be complete until 1914; but he expressed the view that by midsummer 1914, the Germans would seize upon any pretext to go to war. That probable excuse would be some fairly trivial incident, likely some outbreak in the Balkans.*

Lord Castlereagh in Military uniform.

How close was that to an accurate prophecy of when and how the war would start?

On Friday, 14 May 1915, Mr Herbert Day, son of the late Alderman William Day JP and his wife, who lived at Somerfield, was found dead in the river Medway between Tovil and Fairleigh. There were no signs of foul play or any indication that his death had been the result of suicide. One of Herbert's brothers, William Day, was both a councillor and a JP as well as being the principal of Messrs. W. Day and Sons, a well-known firm of Maidstone auctioneers. Another brother, Mr Walter H. Day, was the clerk of the peace for the Maidstone Borough. Herbert had previously been suffering with neurasthenia, an ill-defined condition the symptoms of which included fatigue, headaches, loss of appetite, insomnia, inability to concentrate, and irritability; in short, it was a mild form of depression. Prior to his death he had been in good spirits, in a 'cheerful and hopeful disposition', and been 'making plans for the future', due to his continuing period of good health. A newspaper article about the death stated that he had returned to live in Maidstone having spent some years away and having lived in both Devon and London with his wife, son and daughter. At the inquest, local physician Doctor Southey said that he felt it probable that Mr Day had had some kind of fainting fit causing him to fall into the river. At the coroner's suggestion, the jury returned a verdict of 'Found Drowned'. A check of the census first shows Herbert as a 6-year-old boy in 1871 living at 10 Ashford Road, Maidstone, with his parents William and Ellen, his two brothers William and Walter, and his sister Ellen. William Day senior was shown as being an auctioneer and upholsterer. Fast forward ten years and the family have moved a couple of doors away to 6 Ashford Road and there is an addition to the family in the shape of Gertrude, another sister for Herbert, who is now working as an auctioneer's clerk, presumably with his father's firm. In the census of 1891, Herbert is still living with his parents even though by now he is 26 years of age. The family have now moved to London Road in Maidstone and Herbert is described as an upholsterer. By 1901 Herbert is married to Myra, who is 8 years his junior. They have two children, a son Cyril and a daughter Irene, and are living at 'Waldenhoe' in Maidstone. He is now a maker of 'house furniture' and a cabinet maker and has his own business which has done well enough for him to be able to employ a cook and a housemaid. In 1911 he had become an 'artist' and was living with his mother Ellen at 79 London Road, Maidstone, while Myra is living with her parents in Dashwood Road, Gravesend. Cyril, now 15, is at boarding school in Reading, while sister Irene is at boarding school in Seaton, Devon. The reason for providing all this information is by way of confirming that we are still talking about the same Herbert Day whose body was found in the Medway River. A check of the National Probate Calendar for England and Wales, under the Wills and Administration Index, shows Herbert John Day having died on Friday, 7 May 1915, in Maidstone, but not how he died. It also shows that he left a large sum of money, but not to his wife Myra. Instead he left the entire amount of £36,067 16s 4d to John Hanks Cooper, his brother-in-law, and his brother Walter Hanks Day. His home address, despite what the report of his death said, wasn't actually in Maidstone, but at 6 Melina Place, Middlesex.

The *Kent & Sussex Courier* dated 29 January 1915 included an article about the Kent Education Committee's monthly meeting which took place on Monday, 25 January, at the Sessions House in Maidstone. The meeting took just fifteen minutes to get through the published agenda. The first point on the agenda was a report from the Elementary Education Sub-Committee, that they had given consideration to the question of the safety of children throughout the Kent area in the possible event of a German naval raid on the county's coastline. They had sent letters to all head teachers in the county, especially those situated in coastal towns, advising them to consider the best arrangements for returning children to their homes by safe routes in the event of such raids taking place when their children were either in or on their way to school.

The next point I have read over and over again, but I am still not absolutely certain what it means:

> *The Sub-Committee did not consider it desirable that children under 14 years of age should be employed as monitors unless they had obtained total exemption from compulsory attendance by proficiency. They accordingly recommended that in future the Committee should not appoint as monitors children who obtained exemptions from compulsory attendance by previous good attendance.*

An interesting statistic came up at the meeting in relation to Belgian refugees. With the war still only six months old, there were already a total of 136 Belgian children attending schools throughout the county of Kent. It can only be assumed that a lot of these young children did not initially speak any English so lessons for them must have originally been in French, which in itself must have been somewhat of a strain on a profession that, because of the war, was somewhat understaffed.

On Friday, 26 March 1915, two airmen had a remarkable scrape with death, and thankfully survived. The two men, both serving with the Royal Naval Air Service, were on a training exercise in a monoplane and heading in the direction of Chatham when the engine of their aircraft suddenly and without warning cut out. The pilot tried to keep control of the machine as best he good, but as it was nearing the ground the nose dropped downwards sharply causing it to speed up its dramatic descent. Facing almost certain death, good fortune stepped in to save the day: one of the aircraft's wings clipped a tree, which prevented it from smashing nose first into the ground and flipping over which would have undoubtedly killed both men. They suffered no more than a bit of a shaking and a few facial cuts.

More men died as a result of training accidents during the war than those who were killed in action. The Commonwealth War Graves Commission website shows that by the end of the war a total of 10,656 Commonwealth pilots and crew had been killed, both in action and as a result of training accidents. Denis Winter's book *The First of the Few* quoted a total of 14,166 dead pilots, of which some 8,000 had been killed while undergoing training. The book also spoke of the situation coming to the ears of those in the Houses of Parliament, and that on 20 June 1918, the Home Secretary was asked for an explanation about the ever-increasing losses of airmen. His reply was somewhat offensive: he blamed the pilots themselves, saying, 'discipline after all, is not the eminent quality of youth'. Today, it is staggering to think that these brave men went to war in planes that were predominantly made out of wood and canvas and that the pilots and crews were not allowed to wear parachutes as senior officers believed it would encourage them to abandon a dogfight sooner than they needed to.

The *Birmingham Mail* dated Saturday, 27 March 1915, carried an article about the mistaken identity of a dead soldier which led to extraordinary scenes at a military funeral. The presence of two men in the same battery of the Royal Field Artillery with the exact same name and a similar service number was, with the benefit of hindsight, unfortunate to say the least. On 11 March, Gunner George Webb from Snodland near Maidstone died after falling ill during his initial training in Glasgow. His wife was notified of his passing and obtained a railway pass for her and her mother-in-law. They travelled up to Scotland with George's brother. On their arrival at the hospital in Glasgow they saw a gun carriage outside the mortuary chapel. The hospital chaplain came out to meet them, informing them that they could view the body after the remembrance service that was just about to begin. The service duly over, an attendant removed a sheet which had been covering the dead man's body that was laid out in his coffin. George's mother immediately called out, 'That's not my boy!' Remarkably, her exclamation was taken as that of an overwrought mother consumed with grief and not to be taken seriously. George's wife, his mother and brother were all shown outside just as a group of soldiers entered the chapel by another door to bear the Union Jack-clad coffin out to the waiting gun carriage. As the soldiers carefully lowered the coffin onto the gun carriage, all clearly coming in to view, the brother suddenly exclaimed, 'Why, there's George!' Thankfully for them, it was the other George Webb who had died. The relief for all three of them, mother, wife and brother, must have been palpable. If any of them fainted with the shock of discovering that their loved one was still alive was not recorded in the article. Sadly, as the family of the George Webb who had actually died hadn't been informed that he had died, none of them were at his funeral which went ahead later that day when he was buried at the Western Necropolis cemetery in Glasgow. How dreadful must that have been for the family of the George Smith who had died, to be informed that not only had their loved one died, but that he had already been buried, sadly denying them the opportunity to see him laid to rest and pay their respects. Even when a soldier died back home in the United Kingdom, he was normally buried close to where he had died; very rarely was he sent back to his local parish church to be buried.

The tragic news concerning the death of their son Second Lieutenant Ronald Bluett Winch, who served with the 10th (Royal East and West Kent Yeomanry) Battalion, The Buffs (East Kent Regiment), was received by Lieutenant Colonel George Bluett Winch and his wife

Ethel on 16 April 1915 at their home, Boughton Place, Boughton Monchelsea, near Maidstone. The circumstances of Ronald's death happened in what can only be classed as extremely unusual circumstances, bizarre even. The inquest into his death took place on Monday, 19 April 1915, at Ramsgate General Hospital. PC Simmons, a reserve constable, was standing on East Cliff in Ramsgate at 10.20 on the evening of Friday, 16 April, talking to a sentry on guard duty in the area of the kiosk on the East Cliff, which was immediately adjacent to the sea front. He noticed a bright light coming towards them from the direction of Albion House, which was also noticed by the sentry, who determined that he would stop the vehicle and have the driver of the car switch off his headlights. Constable Simmons shone his torch as the car approached and it stopped. Although they didn't know it at the time, one of the occupants was none other than Lieutenant Colonel George Bluett Winch, with Lieutenant De Laune the driver, who admitted hearing the challenges. Moments later a second vehicle came speeding towards their location. As the vehicle approached, the sentry stepped into the road and shouted loudly three or four times for the car to halt, but it failed to do so, although the driver did dip the vehicle's headlights. Without any prior warning, the sentry fired one round at the car just as it came round a bend in the road, causing it to stop moments later. PC Simmons confirmed that anybody who was driving a vehicle along the seafront at night had to do so with their headlights kept as low as possible. The sentry concerned, Private Finn, who was stationed in the town with the 2nd/7th Battalion, King's Liverpool Regiment, told the court that he had been given orders to stop any suspicious motor vehicles and people. In relation to the incident he said that he shouted 'Halt' loudly a total of four times and when the car failed to stop and drove past his position he opened fire, aiming as best he could for the front offside tyre. After he had fired the single round he heard somebody call out, 'Help, I've been shot.' In his opinion, Private Finn said, there was no other way to stop the vehicle than to fire at it. Private Ainsworth, the other sentry, who was also a member of the King's Liverpool Regiment, stated that he had also verbally thrown a challenge of 'Halt', but to no avail. He did not understand how it was that the driver of the car couldn't have heard the instruction to halt. The medical evidence showed that Private Finn's round had missed the tyre but penetrated the vehicle before entering Lieutenant Winch's back and carrying on into his hip. The bullet exited his body via his stomach causing a wound which turned out to be fatal. The time of his death had been recorded as 4.15 am on the morning of Sunday, 18 April 1915.

Lieutenant Colonel Winch identified the body as that of his son. Ironically at the time of the incident, the two cars were on their way home after a recruitment meeting in the town. He said that he bore Private Finn no ill will, although he was surprised at how soon he had opened fire. The coroner said for the record, that it should be remembered by all concerned that Lieutenant Winch had died for his country with the same relevance as if he had been killed by a German bullet on the Western Front. He also said that Private Finn was also serving his country and was prepared to do his duty when called upon to do so either by order or necessity, whether that was at Ramsgate or on the Western Front. He further acknowledged that the sentry was faced with the problem that if the car did not stop when he challenged it, what was he to do? He made a decision to shoot at the car's wheels in an attempt at stopping it, but unfortunately missed and hit the lieutenant instead.

Lieutenant E.S. Dawes, of the Royal East Kent Mounted Rifles, had been the driver of a second vehicle and gave evidence that although he didn't dispute what either of the sentries had said, he had not heard their challenge, because the car was rather noisy and the hood of the vehicle was open at the time, and that initially he believed the sound of the gunfire was because one of the tyres had burst. Two independent witnesses, Mauris Nauchitel, a man of Russian nationality who lived some distance from the incident, and Herbert Weeks, a postal worker, told the inquest that they had heard the sentries shouting out challenges of 'Halt'. The jury returned a verdict of 'Death from Misadventure', and added their opinion that no blame should be attached to the sentry who fired the fatal shot. They added that if it were necessary to search all vehicles then it would be prudent for the authorities to look at the best possible deployment of sentries and that they themselves should carry lights, ensuring that they could be clearly seen while conducting the stopping of vehicles during the hours of darkness. The members of the jury also expressed their sympathy to Lieutenant Winch's parents on the loss of their son. Lieutenant Winch was buried at St. Peter's Church at Boughton Monchelsea.

According to the 1911 census, the Winche's, despite being only two of them, were living at Boughton Place with eight servants. One of these was Fred Nelson Farley, who was a groom. Fred, aged 38 at the outbreak of the war, enlisted at Maidstone on 15 December 1914 and became Driver 029139 with the Army Service Corps. Eight days later, he arrived in France, remaining there until 22 November the following year. From there he was sent to Salonica where he stayed for the next two and a half years, until 4 June 1918. While there he contracted malaria which, on his return to the UK, resulted in him being admitted to Mill Hill Military Hospital, situated at the Mill Hill Barracks, which could only cater for twelve men at any one time. He remained in England until the middle of October that year, before being sent back to France on 20 October, finally returning home on 11 February 1919, where he was demobilized the next day. He returned to work for Lieutenant Colonel Winch and his wife Ethel at Boughton Place.

The pain of losing a son was something that the Winche's would experience again, this time during the Second World War, when their adopted son, Lieutenant Anthony Desmond Winch, who was serving with the 4th Battalion, Grenadier Guards, was killed by mortar fire near the town of Maastricht in Holland on 24 January 1945.

Sad stories during wartime were not the sole domain of soldiers. The *Whitstable Times & Herne Bay Herald* for Saturday, 29 May 1915, carried the following report:

Maidstone lady killed in Motor Car accident
A lady was killed in the presence of her brother, who was also badly injured, in a motor car accident at Ealing. Two private motor cars, one a light two seater, travelling in opposite directions, collided at the junction of Windsor Road and The Grove. The lighter car overturned, pinning underneath Mr F E Saunders of Ranelagh Road, Ealing, who was driving, and his sister, Mrs Alice M Crosby of

Week Street, Maidstone. Mrs Crosby was killed and her brother severely injured. Mr Saunders was lately tram manager to the Maidstone Corporation.

Another story involved a Mrs Margaret Hannah Neale, who appeared before Mr Justice Darling at Maidstone on Wednesday, 16 June 1915. Her offence, wilful murder. Her victim, her 8-month-old daughter Phyllis. How did she kill her daughter? By cutting her head off. The jury found her guilty of the crime, to which she had confessed, and she was sentenced to death, but she was reprieved on the personal intervention of the Home Secretary.

Alfred Edwin Claud Toke Dooner was a captain with the 1st Battalion, Royal Welsh Fusiliers, and although his death was subsequently recorded as having been on 30 October 1914, initially he was reported as 'missing in action' and it wasn't until the middle of June 1915 that his death was confirmed. He was killed in fighting at Zandvoorde near Ypres and is buried at the Hooge Crater Cemetery, West-Vlaanderen. It was actually the German government who confirmed his death.

Alfred was the third son of Colonel and Mrs Dooner who lived at Ditton Place near Maidstone. He was educated at Tonbridge and the Royal Military College at Sandhurst and had been in the Army since being gazetted as a second lieutenant on 20 September 1911 when he received his commission. He was promoted to the rank of lieutenant on 4 December the following year and became adjutant shortly before the outbreak of the war. While at Sandhurst he won the drill prize, along with coming top of his class in German, a language in which he would eventually become a first class interpreter. He first arrived in Zeebrugge in Belgium on 4 October 1915 with his regiment.

From reports made by both officers and men who fought at Zandvoorde, it was a brutal affair as the Germans endeavoured to get through to Calais. In their way were elements of the British 7th Division who were thinly spread out across a long front. On the right of the Royal Welsh Fusiliers were trenches that were occupied by dismounted British cavalry who were fighting as infantry. So bravely did they fight that it led one officer to describe what he had witnessed as 'one of the finest feats of the war'. Nearly all of them were either killed or wounded before their position was overrun by the attacking German forces. This in turn meant that the right flank of the Royal Welsh Fusiliers part of the line was now open to an attack. Alfred Dooner, having realised the imminent danger his men were now in, ran across open ground through a hail of enemy bullets to reach the company of men to his right. Having passed on his instructions as to what he wanted of them, he began to make his way back to his position and was seen to fall. Lieutenant Colonel Cadogan, who was in overall command of the 1st Battalion, climbed out his trench and ran to his assistance along with Sergeant H. Evans of 'D' Company. They found that Alfred was already dead before making their way quickly back to their lines, but before they got there Cadogan was also shot and killed. The 7th Division had lost more than 80 per cent of its strength in less than a month and the Royal Welsh Fusiliers, who had started out with 31 officers and 1,100 men, had by 30 October 1914 only one officer and 86 men.

Alfred Dooner had been mentioned in despatches by Sir John French in December 1914 for his conspicuous service in the field and at the time of his death was the youngest adjutant in the regular British Army at 22 years of age.

On Saturday, 17 July 1916, Colonel Sir Arthur Boscawen, a Conservative Member of Parliament, paid a visit to Maidstone as part of a recruitment drive for the 10th (Service) Battalion, Royal West Kent Regiment, which had members from all over Kent. Colonel Boscawen was the commanding officer of the regiment's 3rd (Reserve) Battalion.

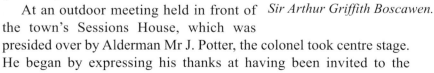

Sir Arthur Griffith Boscawen.

At an outdoor meeting held in front of the town's Sessions House, which was presided over by Alderman Mr J. Potter, the colonel took centre stage. He began by expressing his thanks at having been invited to the meeting and having the opportunity to encourage the men of Maidstone to enlist in the Royal West Kent Regiment, as he felt there was no regiment more worthy of the support of the county's men and no regiment that they would be prouder to join. He said he was extremely proud of the regiment and what its officers and men had already achieved in the war, even more so because it was via the 3rd Reserve Battalion, which he commanded, that other of the regiment's battalions were supplied with much-needed fighting men. Alderman Potter reminded the crowds present that the regiment had always performed in battle to a very high standard, making particular reference to the record of the 'Old 50th' in the Peninsular War some hundred years earlier as they resisted the first onslaught by the French. He compared the heroics of the regiment's forbears with that of their latter day counterparts who had fought so bravely and heroically at the more recent battles at Mons, Neuve Chapelle and at Hill 60, which had enhanced their already stoic reputation to even greater heights. He continued with the rhetorical question,   'Was it not the duty, at this time, of every young man to enlist, who was not otherwise engaged on some other work that was absolutely for the maintenance and benefit of the country?' He reminded everybody present that this was undoubtedly the biggest crisis the country had ever had to face, which meant that these were unequalled and unique times when men needed to take action and be counted. After all it wasn't just Great Britain's future that was at stake but the liberty of the whole of Europe, making the destiny of each reliant on the other. If France and Belgium fell under the weight of the German onslaught, then there was every chance that Britain would be next on the list of countries that Germany would want to conquer. He pointed out that before the war the difference in the populations of Germany and England was some twenty million in their favour, but by conquering France and Belgium, who were both big manufacturing nations, Germany would have an even greater advantage. Mr Potter continued with a patriotic history lesson of bygone eras, a major theme of which was how British soldiers had so often won the day despite overwhelming odds. He spoke with so much passion, fervor and desire in wanting men to enlist, it was almost as if he was on some kind of bonus for every man who subsequently enlisted (which he wasn't). He acknowledged that Kent was doing its bit, but he posed the question, 'Are we doing enough? We are doing a great deal, but we are not doing as much as we could do, and there are men yet shirking, men who don't see why they should go, men who are waiting to be fetched.' He implored Maidstone men to come forward willingly and enlist.

Some men didn't want to go and fight in a war that they had little or no interest in, no matter how passionately Alderman Potter spoke of it. These men weren't shirking, conscientious objectors or even cowards. It has to be remembered that at the time of the First World War a very large percentage of those men who were being asked, cajoled, or embarrassed into enlisting, did not have the right to vote in a general election. They were being told that it was their duty to go off and fight in a war in which they had had no say.

On Wednesday, 4 August 1915, in common with most other towns throughout the nation, Maidstone held a meeting in support of the first anniversary of the outbreak of the war. The Mayor of Maidstone, Councillor W.H. Martin, chaired the meeting. The town's Member of Parliament, Commander C. Bellairs, was in attendance, as was Colonel Ward who represented Mid-Kent in the same capacity, along with numerous other local dignitaries. Speeches were made by some of those present, the theme of their words generally in favour of the war along with a desire to support the government in their continuing efforts until victory had been achieved.

Some found it quite insulting that these men who were showing such support for the war were not the ones who had to, or could, go off and do the fighting, yet they were more than happy to encourage and tell others that they should.

During that first year of the war, the Commonwealth War Graves Commission website shows that a total of 118,976 British and Commonwealth soldiers had been killed or died of their wounds or disease. Of these, at least 122 were men with Maidstone connections.

Maidstone councillor Mr Lawrence Green and his wife Rosalie received the sad news of the sudden and unexpected death of the eldest of their four children, their only daughter Phyllis. She passed away on 3 September 1915 at the relatively young age of 29. She was married with a small child, the family home being at St. Michael's Road, Oaklands, Maidstone. Her husband was Royal Navy Lieutenant Commander Herbert Richardson Stokes, who thankfully survived the war, enabling him to bring up their child. She was buried at Maidstone Cemetery on Tuesday 7 September 1915. The funeral service was conducted by the Vicar of Maidstone, Canon E.H. Hardcastle. Councillor Green and his wife, who also lived in St. Michael's Road, had two of their three sons serving in the war. Their eldest, Robin, who before the war had been an assistant manager in his father's paper mill, had enlisted in the Army, aged nearly 26, on 5 September 1914 at Chatham. His attestation form shows that initially he became a private (1654) with The Buffs (Royal East Kent Regiment) but later changed to the Royal Army Medical Corps where he became private 83596. His address at the time was shown as 49 All Saints, Maidstone. While with the Buffs he got himself into trouble with the military authorities by breaking himself out of his barracks and making himself absent without leave. He faced a military trial on 9 August 1915, was found guilty and sentenced to fourteen days' imprisonment, but he was not dismissed from the service. He had four further incidents of misconduct recorded on his Army service record, most of which resulted in him being confined to barracks. On 3 March 1916 he was transferred to the Royal Army Medical Corps, where six months later he was admitted to the Queen Alexandra Military Hospital Extension with an unspecified ailment. He remained there for fifteen days while receiving treatment. On 10 September 1916 he married Evelyn Mary Goatley at the All Saints Parish Church in Wakefield, Yorkshire. Strangely enough their wedding certificate showed that they were both residing at the White Horse Hotel in Wakefield. On 12 May 1917 he was discharged from the Army so that he could join the Royal Naval Air Service, becoming a mechanic (F203238), second class. There was a note on his Naval service record that the middle finger of his left hand was missing. He was finally demobilized on 29 January 1919, having completed 4 years and 4 months' service.

The Greens' other son who saw service during the First World War and also survived was Thomas Littleton Green who served with both the 1/1st (Kent) Battalion, the Kent Cyclist Battalion (who between

March 1916 and November 1919 were stationed in India) and also the Royal Flying Corps.

The *Kent & Sussex Courier* for 8 October 1915 included an article about recruitment which, if it was not about such a serious topic, could be described as hilarious. On Saturday, 2 October 1915, a recruiting rally was held at Maidstone, the intention of which was to encourage young men to enlist in the Royal West Kent Regiment. The main speaker at the rally was Lieutenant Colonel Anthony Wood Martyn, who was the commanding officer of the 10th (Kent County) Battalion, Royal West Kent Regiment, for the years 1915, 1916 and 1917.

Lieutenant Colonel Anthony Wood Martyn DSO OBE.

Details of the award of Martyn's DSO appeared in the *London Gazette* on 25 August 1917, his OBE on 3 June 1919. He was also awarded the Belgian medals, the Order of Leopold and the Croix de Guerre. During his speech he said the following:

> *I have heard that the Royal West Kents were in the thick of the recent fighting on the Western Front, and that they had lost practically a Battalion in casualties. If the County Battalion was up to full strength it ought to be ready in November to go out and take the places of the men who have been killed.*

I was always under the impression that if you were trying to sell an idea to somebody, regardless of what it was, or how much you did or did not believe in it, you needed to put a positive spin on it for it to have any chance of being seen and accepted in a positive light. I would therefore respectfully suggest that telling a crowd of men who you wanted to convince to enlist in a particular regiment, that they had just lost an entire battalion of perhaps 1,000 men, and that they could soon be out in France as their replacements, was simply not a good selling point. Sometimes, people can just be too honest.

All elements of British society were feeling the effects of the war in one way or another. Education was no exception. According to figures compiled by the Commonwealth War Graves Commission, at least seventy-eight men who were killed or died during the war had been teachers in their civilian life. There would have been more who had been wounded, some who were unable to return to the profession. Hundreds of teachers went off to war.

With this in mind, F.W. Crook, secretary of the Kent Education Committee, submitted the following letter which appeared in the *Kent & Sussex Courier* on Friday, 26 November 1915:

> *Wanted. Men and women of sufficient health, of good education, and of some teaching experience, for employment in Kent in Elementary and Secondary schools and Technical Institutes, to fill the places of teachers desiring to join HM Forces.*
>
> *Application to be made to the under-signed, stating age, qualifications, and whether willing to serve in any district as directed, or only in some particular district.*
>
> *Salaries in accordance with qualifications.*
> *Men must be ineligible for Military Service.*
> *By order of the Committee*
> *F W Crook*
> *Secretary*
> *Sessions House*
> *Maidstone*
> *16 November 1915.*

The chances are that this request ultimately attracted more women than it did men, as there would likely be fewer men of sufficient education with the required teaching experience available, especially with conscription just around the corner.

On 10 December 1915, a slightly bizarre article appeared in the *Kent & Sussex Courier* about the Mayor of Maidstone being in communication with the War Office over a captured German artillery piece. For some reason the decision had been made for the Mayor to contact the War Office in the hopes of securing a captured German gun so that it could be presented to the town like a trophy, similar to one already in place at the time in Canterbury. There was also talk of the nearby town of Tunbridge Wells doing the same, and numerous other towns up and down the country had done similar. Although this was no doubt done with the best of intentions in mind, it strikes me that it was somewhat odd. Between the outbreak of the war in August 1914 and the end of 1915, at least 167 men with Maidstone connections had been killed in action or died as a result of the war; that's nearly ten every month. How would the families of these men have felt about having such a visual reminder of their sad loss in the shape of a German gun placed in the middle of their town? I can only imagine that their suffering would have been made worse.

CHAPTER 4

1916
The Realisation

By now the phrase 'It'll all be over by Christmas' had worn somewhat thin. The Christmases of 1914 and 1915 had come and gone and still there was no sign of an end to the bloody war. It would be over by Christmas, eventually, but nobody could say which Christmas that would be!

The village of Detling is situated to the north-east of Maidstone and during the First World War it was the home to a Royal Naval Air Station. The Army's Royal Flying Corps received its royal warrant on 13 April 1912 and the Sopwith Aviation Company obtained its first order for military aircraft from the British government five months later. The Royal Naval Air Service came into being on 1 July 1914, one month before the outbreak of the First World War. On 1 April 1918 it was amalgamated with the Royal Flying Corps, which was the flying wing of the British Army, and together they became the Royal Air Force.

RNAS Detling received a Sopwith Type 806 Gunbus pusher aircraft on 3 January 1916. It had been built under licence by Robey & Sons of Lincoln, then delivered to Sopwith's factory in Kingston. That same day it was delivered to the RNAS station at Detling, sustaining damage to its chassis and propeller; the aircraft had crash-landed, the culprit being the suddenly not so popular Flight Sub-Lieutenant D.E. Smith.

RNAS No.1 Squadron 1914.

There were three major battles of 1916: Verdun and the Somme on land, and the Battle of Jutland at sea.

The Battle of Jutland, the largest sea battle of the war, took place over two days, 31 May and 1 June. The British threw a total of 155 vessels in to the affray, which included 28 battleships, against 99 vessels from Germany, 16 of which were battleships. Although Britain managed to contain the German fleet, she lost more ships that Germany did and suffered more than twice as many men killed.

Six Maidstone men were killed during the battle. Boy, First Class (J/43059) Reginald Walter Ball, aged 16, was born in Maidstone. He died on 31 May 1916 while serving on board HMS *Indefatigable*. His name is commemorated on the Plymouth Naval Memorial. Just after 4pm on 31 May 1916, in a gunnery exchange with the German vessel SMS *Von der Tann*, HMS *Indefatigable* was struck by three shells which put her out of the battle but also detonated one of her magazines. A short while later she was struck by a further shell fired by the *Von der Tann* which ripped her apart when another of her magazines exploded. She sunk almost immediately, with the loss of 1,019 of her crew. There were only two known survivors.

Edward Pickett Chapman was 52 years of age, having been born in Maidstone in 1864. He was a stoker 1st class (49415) and was also one of the crew of *Indefatigable.* His name is commemorated on the Chatham Naval Memorial.

James Henry Fever was 45 years of age and was also from Maidstone. He too was a stoker 1st class (151681) on board HMS *Indefatigble.*

John Porter Gibbs was 27 years of age and a private (CH/16102) in the Royal Marine Light Infantry, serving on board HMS *Chester* when he was killed in action on 31 May 1916. His home was at Chart Road, Chart Sutton, Maidstone. His name is commemorated on the Chatham Naval Memorial.

At just before 5.30 pm on 31 May 1916, HMS *Chester*, part of the 3rd Battle Cruiser Squadron, came in to contact with ships of the German's light cruiser squadron, 2nd Scouting Group. Within five minutes of the initial contact *Chester* had three of her guns knocked out, but was not done for. Although badly damaged, she survived the contact and made it to safety. Sadly, thirty-one of her crew, including John Gibbs and Victoria Cross recipient John Cornwell, were killed.

William Wright was 32 years of age when he was killed while serving on board the battlecruiser HMS *Queen Mary* as an officer's cook 1st class (363182). He was a married man who, along with his wife Alice, had lived at 41 Union Street, Maidstone, before he had gone off to war. His name is commemorated on the Chatham Naval Memorial.

HMS *Queen Mary* was already a veteran of the war, having seen action at the Battle of Heligoland and during the raid on Scarborough by ships of the Imperial German Navy. Jutland would be her third major engagement. At just before 3.45 pm on 31 May 1916 she found herself engaged with the German vessel SMS *Seyditz.* Both vessels pounded each other with their big guns, both scoring hits with two of their shells. In the mayhem of battle, SMS *Derfflinger* also began engaging the *Queen Mary*, striking her with a further two shells, one of which detonated one of her magazines, the explosion breaking the

John Travers Cornwell VC, 1915.

ship in two. Out of a full complement of 1,284, there were only 18 survivors.

Charles John Wintour was 44 years of age and lived at Pickering Cottage, Loose, Maidstone. He was a captain serving in the Royal Navy when he was killed in action on 31 May 1916. During the battle he was on board HMS *Tipperary* which was the Flotilla Leader for the 4th Destroyer Flotilla. Her job was to support the Grand Fleet by making torpedo attacks on the German fleet. While doing so she was struck by the guns of the battleship SMS *Westfalen* and sunk with the loss 185 of her crew. There were only 12 survivors. Captain Wintour's name is commemorated on the Portsmouth Naval Memorial.

Verdun was the longest single battle of the first World War, lasting for nearly ten months. Estimates of casualties vary greatly. It is known that the French used 1,140,000 soldiers during the battle, the Germans a similar number, 1,250,000. By the end of the battle France had suffered between 315,000 and 542,000 casualties, of which an estimated 156,000 to 162,000 had been killed. As for the Germans their casualties were estimated to be between 281,000 and 431,000. Of these 143,000 were killed. This meant that collectively there were an estimated 70,000 casualties each and every month of the conflict, truly staggering figures.

The Battle of Verdun was linked with the Battle of the Somme, as the latter, which was a British offensive against the Germans, was in part to try to take the pressure off of the French at Verdun and cause Germany to remove some of the troops that she had thrown in to battle against the French. British troops were not involved in the Battle of Verdun.

The Battle of the Somme began on 1 July 1916 and continued until 18 November 1916. On one side was the German Army, while on the Allied side were troops from France, the United Kingdom, Southern Rhodesia, South Africa, New Zealand, Newfoundland, India, Canada, Bermuda and Australia. Which side won is open to debate.

The battle was preceded by a week-long, twenty-four-hour-a-day artillery bombardment of German defensive positions, but it was ineffective. Instead of being able to walk freely across no man's land towards a scattered enemy, British soldiers walked head first into German machine gun fire. The first day of the battle saw Britain and her Allies sustain 57,470 casualties, of which an estimated 20,000 were killed.

As far as I have been able to find out, nobody from Maidstone was killed during the first day of the Somme. Approximately 116 Maidstone

A young German soldier at the Somme.

men died during the whole battle, but this is based purely on dates; it includes those who had been wounded beforehand and died during the battle, and it excludes those who were wounded during the battle and died later.

The year had opened with the Military Service Act 1916 coming into being as of 27 January which, in short, meant conscription. For the first time ever, men throughout the United Kingdom could legally be required by their country to enlist in the Army and go and fight in the war. Along with the Defence of the Realm Act 1914, it was possibly one of the most controlling and powerful pieces of legislation ever brought in by the British Government. As was usual, the Act had a varied number of ifs, buts and maybes attached to it. It included all British males who on 15 August 1915 were ordinarily resident in Great Britain and who were at least 19 years of age, but who had not reached the age of 41, and who on 2 November 1915 were either single or a widower who did not have any children. There was also a list of exceptions, these were:

(1) British men who as a matter of course were usually resident in a Commonwealth country, or were resident in Britain only for their education or other special purpose.
(2) Existing members of the regular, reserve or territorial forces who were liable for foreign service, or who were, in the opinion of the Army Council, not suitable for foreign service.
(3) Men serving in the Navy or Royal Marines or who were recommended for exemption by the Admiralty.
(4) Men in Holy Orders or regular ministers of any religious denomination.
(5) Men who had served with the military or Navy and been discharged on grounds of ill health or termination of service.
(6) Men who held a certificate of exemption or who had offered themselves for enlistment since 4 August 1914 but been rejected.

Added on top of this list was then another one which provided a list of reasons that men could use to claim an exemption from having to undergo military training. To do this a man had to make an application at an appointed time and date to a local Tribunal, which could consist of between 5 and 25 members, for the issue of a Certificate of Exemption:

(1) A certificate of exemption can be issued if it is expedient in the national interests that he should be engaged in other work, or, if he is being educated or trained for any other work, that he should continue, or
(2) If serious hardship would ensue owing to his exceptional financial or business obligations or domestic position, or
(3) Ill health or infirmity, or
(4) Conscientious objection to the undertaking of combatant service.

The last of these exemptions was carefully worded and didn't say 'military' service, it distinctly said 'combatant' service. This one word gave the authorities the ability to turn down lots of appeals from conscientious objectors, because although it meant that if men could prove they had a long standing genuine conscientious objection, such as on religious grounds, then although the authorities could not place them with an infantry or artillery unit, they could still be placed with such units as the Labour Corps, the Non-Combatant Corps or as stretcher bearers with the Royal Army Medical Corps, or the Friends Ambulance Unit. Those who refused to join one these units then had somewhat of a dilemma, because once they had been called up they came under military law and were dealt with accordingly. This could mean a court martial and a prison sentence.

Some 16,000 men became conscientious objectors as a result of conscription and refused to fight. Thirty-six of these men were actually sentenced to death, but had their sentences commuted to prison sentences, usually with hard labour.

Maidstone was involved in the conscientious objection issue, as many of those who refused to have anything to do with the war in any capacity at all found themselves held in Maidstone Prison.

One such man was Harold Shoebridge Hoad, who spent time in Maidstone Prison for being a conscientious objector. During his time in prison his health deteriorated, so much so that he was discharged from the Army in May 1918. Four months later, on 7 September 1918, he was dead. It was a sad irony that the war he refused to be part of still was ultimately responsible for taking his life. Harold was born on 30 May 1896 at Wittersham in Kent to parents Jonathon and Annie, who had eight other children, six sons and two daughters. He married Fanny on 27 December 1909 at Wittersham Parish Church and their daughter was born in Boughton Montchelsea on 11 June 1910, indicating that Fanny was either three months pregnant at the time of the wedding or that their daughter Phyllis was born three months prematurely. Harold has a British Army Pension Record which shows he was Private 17010 and served with the Royal West Kent Regiment. The first entry on the Statement of Services page in his record shows that on 28 and 29 July 1916, he was in custody:

> *In custody of Civil Powers fined 40/-. Handed over to Military authority at Maidstone Police Court.*

He was deemed to have joined on 29 July 1916, but he didn't have an 'Enrolment Paper', only a 'Record of Service'. On 31 July he refused to undergo a medical examination and was posted to the 3rd Battalion, Royal West Kent Regiment. The next entry is dated 1 August 1916 and records that he was awaiting trial by a district court martial for when on active service disobeying a lawful command given to him by his superior officer. It then states he was sentenced to six months, but this has been crossed out. It then reads:

> *To Maidstone Civil Prison 14 August 1916, sentence amended to read 112 days hard labour, 17 days remitted. Authority War Office letter.*

The next entry shows him having committed the exact same breach of the Army Discipline Code on 13 November 1916. He is again put before a district court martial on 5 December 1916 and is sentenced to two years' imprisonment with hard labour, but one year and twenty-one days of the sentence was remitted as a result of a letter sent by the War Office. He was sent to Maidstone Civil Prison on 11 December 1916 to serve his sentence.

On 9 May 1917 Harold was yet again awaiting trial for disobeying a lawful command given to him by his superior officer. His trial was by district court martial on 15 May 1917 where he was sentenced to a further two years' imprisonment with hard labour. This in turn was mitigated to read twelve months with hard labour. The authority for this reduction was once again a letter sent from the War Office. On 6 June 1917 this was further remitted to fifty-three days' imprisonment with hard labour.

Even after all of the time that was taken off of his numerous sentences, he still ended up spending 1 year and 239 days incarcerated in Maidstone Prison.

On 27 March 1918 he was once again on trial before a district court martial

> *for disobeying in such a manner as to show a willful defiance of authority a lawful command given personally by his superior officer in the execution of his office.*
> *Finding:- Guilty.*
> *Sentence:- To undergo two years imprisonment with hard labour. Confirmed and signed at Chatham by General Officer Commanding Special Reserve Brigade 28 March 1918.*

After Harold had served just forty-seven days he was released from prison and discharged from the Army for no longer being physically fit for war service because of tuberculosis of the lungs, but he would still be liable to be sent a statutory order on 13 May 1919 requiring him to present himself for medical re-examination under the Military Service (Review of Exceptions) Act 1917. This would sadly be an appointment that he would not keep.

His time spent in prison had seen him incarcerated at Wormwood Scrubs, Rochester, Maidstone, and Fort Horsted. From the latter he was transferred to Fort Pitt Military Hospital because of the worsening condition of his health. This is where the medical report about him was written.

On being discharged, Harold was awarded an Army pension, mainly because although the date of the original ailment was unknown, the Army conceded that it had probably begun since his enlistment. This is later contradicted in the same report when it states that his condition was not aggravated by any service condition, but probably by his occupation as a stonemason.

The Army Medical Board report was completed on 22 April 1918, three weeks before he was discharged from the Army. It is signed by Captain H.A. Hancock of the Royal Army Medical Corps.

Harold died on 7 September 1918. Even though he had been discharged from the Army before he died, but as a result of an illness which he had picked up while serving in the Army, his name is not recorded on the Commonwealth War Graves Commission website.

The *Kent & Sussex Courier* dated 2 June 1916 included a couple of stories of Maidstone men involved in the war.

John Marshall Youngman was a lieutenant in the 9th Battalion, East Surrey Regiment, and it was reported that he had recently been awarded the Military Cross. Lieutenant Youngman, who was holding a temporary rank, was given his award for conspicuous gallantry. He volunteered to lead a party taking much-needed ammunition to the front lines, under heavy fire, and upon his arrival helped to restore the situation. He acted with great coolness and courage in the counter-attack, whereby a portion of the trench which had been lost was recovered.

He was the eldest son of Mr John Henry Youngman, a corn merchant, and his wife Adelaide Edith of Bower Hill House, 104 Tonbridge Road, Maidstone. He was also a grandson of the late Mr George Youngman, formerly a well-known personality in the town. Before the war he had been a student, boarding at Dover College.

Sadly, less than a month after his award Youngman was dead, killed in action on 23 June 1916. He was 20 years of age and is buried at the Dranoutre Military Cemetery, West-Vlaanderen, Belgium. His service medals were applied for by his father on 17 November 1919.

John Arthur Ruck was 20 years of age and a second lieutenant in the Royal Flying Corps when he was killed in a flying accident on 25 May 1916 in the skies over Thetford, Norfolk in only his third solo flight, having qualified as a pilot earlier that month. His aircraft crashed into a field, turned somersault and caught fire.

Before the war John had been a medical student at the London Hospital and had been on medical duties in Unit 5, Boulogne Red Cross, earlier in the war. He took his commission in the Royal Flying Corps from the Artists' Rifles and had undergone his pilot training at Oxford before going to Norwich. His funeral took place on Tuesday, 30 May 1916, and began with the coffin, draped in in a Union Jack flag, being slowly conveyed through the town on a horse-drawn hearse. Members of his family along with colleagues from the Royal Flying Corps followed behind. The body was laid to rest at Maidstone cemetery.

John had two brothers, Dennis Alfred Walter who was two years his senior, and Sydney who was three years his junior. Dennis served with the Cheshire Regiment during the war as a lieutenant, survived the war, and died in South Africa in 1948.

John's parents, Morris Alfred Ruck, an ironmonger, and Augusta, lived at Weavering Grange, near Maidstone.

In a time of war on the home front, one of the biggest issues, besides worrying about loved ones off doing the fighting, are the shortages. Foodstuffs are the most obvious concern, especially as some items are imported rather than home grown. The other item is of course fuel, especially petrol.

Mr Francis Chambers of Chart Sutton, Maidstone, was a fruit grower, who grew his produce across four small farms. In August 1916 he wrote a letter to the *Times* newspaper concerning his frustration at having had his fuel allowance capped at what he saw as an unworkable level:

> *I am a fruit grower who markets several hundred tons of fruit in the year. I am also an invalid who cannot walk any long distance, or cycle without considerable pain and exhaustion. I have four small farms, several miles apart, which I have to visit daily in a motor-car, which I am obliged to keep for the purpose. I make a return that I require 32 gallons of petrol a month. This precious department allots me eight. This stops my business dead. I have written letters explaining everything. The*

department sends a printed form, regretting that it cannot increase the allowance, etc. So my fruit, which is well known in Covent Garden, is of no concern either to the country or to this all powerful department.

Are we not marvelously and efficiently governed? If I obtain a gallon from a dealer we are both threatened with one hundred pound fines or six months' imprisonment.

On the surface it did appear to be somewhat of a strange situation. Here was Mr Chambers, who by the sound of things was a major fruit producer, a foodstuff much needed throughout the nation, and a government department wouldn't allow him sufficient petrol effectively to continue his business and if he tried to purchase more he faced a hefty fine or imprisonment.

In 1916 Mr Chambers was 60 years of age and besides being a fruit grower he was also a clerk in holy orders. He lived at Lested Lodge, Chart Sutton, Maidstone. He had been married to his wife Frances for twenty-five years. They had three children, two daughters, Gladys and Olive, and a son, Wilfred.

The letter which Francis wrote to the *Times* also appeared in the *Kent & Sussex Courier* on Friday, 25 August 1916. Sadly, Francis's son Wilfred, who was a lieutenant in the 13th Battalion on attachment from the 11th Battalion, East Surrey Regiment, was killed in action on 18 August 1916, just a week before the letter was posted, and quite possibly before Mr and Mrs Chambers had heard about his death. At the time of his death, Wilfred was 22 years of age. He is buried at the Loos British Cemetery in the Pas-de-Calais region of France.

The *Chelmsford Chronicle* dated 10 November 1916 reported the death of Gunner (126826) Walter Fuller of the Royal Field Artillery, 15th Brigade. He was the son of Rev. Walter Fuller of Maidstone, formerly vicar of the Congregational Church at Great Stambridge. Gunner Fuller had been wounded in action and died on 18 October 1916 in hospital while still in France. He is buried at the St. Sever Cemetery in Rouen.

As Christmas 1916 approached, there was a sad reminder of just how frail life could be and how suddenly it could come to an end. On

Sunday, 10 December, a 72-year-old widower departed this life, not because of the war but at his own hand. Mr John Bailey, a lodger at 36 Tovil Hill in Maidstone, had been in poor health in the weeks leading up to his death and had been in the local infirmary where he had been treated for a breakdown. He had been employed by Maidstone Corporation as a road cleaner, a job he had been doing for some thirteen years. He was found at the bottom of Tovil Hill near to where he was living, in a shed that was used by the Corporation's roadmen. He had hung himself.

On Wednesday, 13 December, Alderman Mr Stephen Britt JP of Church Street, Maidstone, passed away after suffering an attack of bronchitis. He was 89 years of age and would have made his 90th birthday later in the month. He had taken to his bed only a matter of days before his death with the same ailment, a complaint to which he had been subject for many years. Despite his advanced years he had retained his faculties and vigor to the end. Although born in Rye, Sussex, he moved to Maidstone in 1853 and had lived there for the rest of his life, which had been something of a distinguished one. He had been a member of Maidstone Town Council since 1886 as a staunch Conservative. He was appointed a local magistrate in 1900. In 1904 he became an alderman, and the following year he was appointed Mayor of Maidstone.

On Thursday, 14 December, Mr Richard James Ralston JP of Springfield, Maidstone, and who was relatively well known locally, passed away. He was 78 years of age. Twenty-five years earlier he had been the head of the firm of Messrs. W. and R. Balston of Springfield Mill, the country's leading hand-made paper mill and well known internationally for its Whatman papers. Mr Balston was for a while a member of the Maidstone Town Council, a trustee of the Ophthalmic Hospital, as well as being a justice of the peace for the county. In 1894 he served in the office of the High Sheriff for Kent. The circumstances of his death were not explained.

CHAPTER 5

1917
Seeing it Through

While everyday life continued for the people of Maidstone during 1917, the war was still going on with a vengeance. The feelings of euphoria which had started with the outbreak of war, and continued for a period of time into 1915, had long since been replaced with a longing for the war to end. But this wasn't necessarily what the politicians wanted. They now strove for a victory over Germans once and for all, no matter what the cost might be in human life, pain and suffering.

Using figures recorded on the Commonwealth War Graves Commission website, 294,000 British and Commonwealth servicemen died in 1917, making it by far the worst year of the war. Here is a month by month break down of the figure:

January – 10,505
February – 15,939
March – 15,001
April – 45,300
May – 27,873
June – 20,860
July – 23,616
August – 28,050
September – 24,408

October – 39,624
November – 26,352
December – 17,065

As can be clearly seen, the worst month for fatalities was April, which saw noticeable battles take place, at Arras, Vimy Ridge, Aisne, Gaza, Shiala, Istabalut, and the Battle of the Boot. Throughout the month of April there were four days where the death toll of British and Commonwealth forces was significantly raised. These were:

9 April – 7,506
11 April – 3,214
23 April – 5,030
28 April – 3,406

These were four days of the Battle of Arras, during which a total of 19,156 men were killed. Arras was a British offensive against German defensive positions that were set up in and around Arras on the Western Front. The operation took place between 9 April and 16 May 1917 and at its end was recorded as being a British victory with what were called 'significant advances', even though the efforts to gain those advances resulted in approximately 30,000 more British casualties than German ones.

How does this relate to Maidstone? That came in the form of casualties. As best as I have been able to establish, there were at least fourteen Maidstone men killed during the fighting in and around Arras, and their names are commemorated on the Arras Memorial. There are a possible further seventeen other Maidstone men who also fell during the battle. I will look at some of these in a bit more detail.

Edward Jessie Bodiam was born in Boxley, Kent in 1884. During the war he enlisted and became a private (G/40358) in the 16th Battalion, Duke of Cambridge's Own (Middlesex) Regiment which was part of the 29th Division and the 18th Army Corps. He was 31 years of age when it is believed that he died of his wounds on 23 April 1917.

The war diaries for the 16th Battalion, Middlesex Regiment, show that after having being relieved from their position in the early hours of 23 April by the 1st Battalion, King's Own Scottish Borderers and the 1st Battalion, Royal Irish Rifles, they then marched to a position between Orange Hill and Monchy. The entry for 23 April 1917 reads as follows:

> *23 noon*
>
> *Battalion comes under orders of General Officer Commanding 88th Brigade, and during the day the disposition becomes as follows:- HQ, N, 12A. 5.3: B Company in junction SPRING, PICK and SHOVEL TRENCHES. A Company strong points 0.7.B.6.3 to 0.8.A.0.7. D Company, southern end of SHRAPNEL TRENCH. C Company, 2 platoons, 0.8.b.0.2 to trench to south of that point. C Company, 2 platoons, 0.7.B.8.6.*
>
> *B Company brings heavy Lewis Gun fire on Hostile counter attack on Copse at 0.8.B.0.2.*
>
> *6pm, Battalion again comes under orders of General Officer Commanding 86th Infantry Brigade.*
>
> *Battalion is ordered to take over SHRAPNEL TRENCH, 0.2.C.2.0 to 0.2.A.3.2. Owing to the few remaining hours of darkness, this was not done.*

There is no mention in the war diaries for that day of any officers or men being killed, confirming that Edward must have died of his wounds received earlier in the battle. There is a collective entry for the dates 15 to 18 April which shows that one officer was killed in action and that another was wounded. For the same period of time, it shows that 7 'other ranks' were killed, a further 59 of them were wounded, with 3 more missing.

Bodiam had originally served with the 3rd Battalion, Royal Sussex Regiment. Before the war he had earned a living as a gardener – soldiering couldn't have been more different from his civilian job. His parents Edward and Sarah Bodiam lived at Otham Mill Cottage, Maidstone. He had a younger brother Ivan who does not appear to have served during the war. Edward's widow Fanny lived at the Keeper's Cottage, Upper Wilmington in Maidstone.

Lewis Alfred Brisley was 26 years of age and a private (47469) in the 23rd (Tyneside Scottish) Battalion, Northumberland Fusiliers, when he was reported missing in action on 29 April 1917 and was subsequently presumed to have been killed on that date. His home address was the cutely named Rabbits Cross Farm, Chart Sutton, Maidstone.

Alfred Lewis Chapman was 19 years of age and a private (L/10789) in the 1st Battalion, Queen's Own (Royal West Kent Regiment) when he was killed in action on 10 April 1917. He was the son of Mrs A. Chapman of 11 Prattling Street, Aylesford, Maidstone.

Herbert Arthur Diprose was born in late November 1898 and was baptised on 4 December 1898 in Maidstone. He was only 19 years of age and a lance corporal (G/24691) in the 6th Battalion, Queen's Own (Royal West Kent Regiment) when he was killed in action on 12 May 1917. Herbert had apparently enlisted in 1914, which if correct would mean that he was only 16 years of age when he did so.

The war diaries for the 6th Battalion, Queen's Own (Royal West Kent Regiment), for 12 May 1917 record the following:

Severe hostile shelling of BAYONET and SCABBARD trenches, in response to the 6th Queen's attack. Last Barrage at 9pm consisting mainly of 8" & 5.9s. 2nd Lieut. B. Keats wounded, 8 other ranks killed, 4 other ranks wounded. Relieved before dawn by 6th Battalion Buffs. Battalion moved back to Sunken Road, known as LANCER LANE.

Herbert's parents, Albert Charles and Rosina Diprose, lived at 1 Charles Street, Maidstone, with their five other children, sons Leonard, Edward, George, and Douglas, and their daughter Gwendoline.

Leonard Albert Diprose was two years older than Herbert. Before he joined the Army he was a railway clerk for South East Counties Railway. He was attested four months before the outbreak of the war when he was 17 years of age on 24 April 1914 at Maidstone, although he wasn't called up until 5 August 1914. He became a private in the Kent Brigade Company, Army Service Corps, which was a Territorial unit, before joining the regular Army on 27 November 1914 at Sittingbourne, and becoming private 038390 in the Army Service Corps. He first arrived in France on 21 December 1914 where he remained until 11 November 1915. What happened to him for the next couple of months is not clear from his service record, although we know that he arrived in Salonica on 12 January 1916 on board HMHS *Itora* after a journey that took ten days and that on his arrival he became part of the 81st Infantry Brigade. His service record shows that he later transferred to the Royal Engineers on 3 August 1918 where he became Sapper 297214 and was used on clerical duties. The reason he was used in this capacity rather than as an infantry soldier was because at his initial medical examination it was discovered that he had flat feet and, although not bad enough to exclude him from military service, it undoubtedly prevented his use as a frontline infantry soldier. He left Salonica on 3 March 1919 and arrived back in the UK twelve days later. He was demobilized a month later on 15 April 1919 having served in the Army for nearly five years.

Wilfred Fletcher was 24 years of age and a rifleman (S/28614) in the 13th Battalion, Rifle Brigade, when he was killed in action on 11 April 1917. His widow Ellen lived in Maidstone Road, Lenham, Maidstone. Wilfred was one of four children and the only son born to James and Mary Fletcher in Rochdale, Lancashire.

William Edward Norris was 34 years of age and a private (G/12738) in the 7th Battalion, Royal Sussex Regiment when he was killed in action on the first day of the Battle of Arras, on 9 April 1917. He has no known grave, but his name is commemorated on the Arras Memorial. His widow Alice lived at Prospect Place, Church Street, Boughton Monchelsea, Maidstone.

Sidney Julius Parker was 19 years of age and a private (G/18762) in the 6th Battalion, The Buffs (East Kent Regiment) when he was killed on the first day of the battle, 9 April 1917. His parents, Stephen and Eliza Parker, lived at 16 Boxly Road, Maidstone, with their four other sons, George, who was the eldest, Ernest, Frederick and Walter, and daughters Maud and Gertrude.

Ernest Stephen Parker, who was some fourteen years older than Sidney, served as a private (G/18622) with the 2nd/4th Battalion,

Queen's Own (Royal West Surrey Regiment) in Egypt during the First World War, having previously served as a private (7002) with the 8th Battalion, Middlesex Regiment. Ernest was killed in action on 27 December 1917, making the year an unforgettable one for his parents, but sadly for the wrong reasons. He was buried in the Jerusalem War Cemetery.

Frederick Robert Parker enlisted on 10 November 1914 at Woolwich, but unfortunately other than the half-burnt front page, his Army service record did not survive. But he survived the war after having served with the Army Service Corps in a Territorial unit as Private T3/024047 and then with the King's Own Royal Lancaster Regiment as Private 28379, having first arrived in France on 18 July 1915.

Job Senior was at 40 years of age, one of the oldest to be killed. He was a private (44206) in the 27th (Tyneside Irish) Northumberland Fusiliers when he fell, also on the first day of the battle. Initially he had been reported as missing in action. Before the war Job had been a labourer and prior to moving to Maidstone he had lived and worked in Hull, having been born in Holmfirth in 1878. It was his wife Emma who was the Kent connection and together they lived at Milton Cottages, Butchers Lane, Mereworth, Maidstone.

Leonard Startup was 33 years of age and a corporal (22823) in the 1st Battalion, Northumberland Fusiliers, when he was killed in action on 3 May 1917. He had enlisted at Guildford in Surrey. The battalion's war diaries for 3 May 1917 record the following information:

A few minutes after ZERO, the enemy put a heavy barrage on the positions occupied by the Battalion, and the leading Companies advanced to try and get in front of it. On reaching the FRONT LINE it was found that the rear wave of the leading Battalion had not yet left, on their leaving, so the leading two Companies of the Battalion advanced with them but owing to the heavy fire it was found impossible to do so, and after several attempts to, it was decided to dig in and improve our original front line. During the attack the Battalion casualties amounted to 7 officers and about 110 other ranks. List of officers and detailed account of the action attached. Battalion HQ was in the Red House at the NW corner of Monchy and was heavily shelled throughout the day. The night passed quietly.

Leonard was one of the large number of men of the battalion who were killed that day. His parents, James and Eliza Startup, lived at 2 Heath Cottages, Tonbridge Road, Maidstone.

Charles Picton Stevens was 41 years of age and a private (G/40972) in the 4th Battalion, Middlesex Regiment, when he was killed in action on 28 April 1917. His widow Laura Ella and their two children, daughter Laura and son Charles, lived at 19 Cross Street, Maidstone.

Frank Venton was 25 years of age and a private (L/9181) in the 7th Battalion, The Buffs (East Kent Regiment), when he was killed in action on 3 May 1917. His mother Mrs E. Venton lived at 66 James Street, Maidstone.

Thomas William White was 32 years of age and a private (25668) in the 8th Battalion, East Surrey Regiment, when he was killed in action on 1 May 1917. He had originally enlisted in the Army at their recruiting office at Maidstone. Prior to enlisting he had worked in a local paper mill which was one of the major employers in the town. His widow Emily Sarah and their daughter Hilda lived at 216 Upper Fant Road, Maidstone; prior to that they had lived at 74 Upper Fant Road.

Edwin Bert Wightwick was 39 years of age and a private (G/12992) in the 7th Battalion, Royal Sussex Regiment, when he was killed in action on the first day of the battle, 9 April 1917. Before he had enlisted in the Army he had been a boot repairer in Maidstone. His widow Emily Matilda and their young son Cecil lived at Park View, Loose, Maidstone.

The following seventeen men I believe were also killed or died because of their involvement in the fighting during the Battle of Arras. As the battle took place over a long front, not all of the men were buried in the same cemetery, or their names commemorated on the same war memorial.

Henry Anstey was 29 years of age and a second lieutenant in the 7th Battalion, Rifle Brigade. He was killed in action during fighting on 11 April 1917 and is buried at the Tigris Lane Cemetery at Wancourt. His widow Dorothy lived at Aberglaslyn, Loose, Maidstone.

Hubert Percival Baker was 27 years of age and a bugler in the 38th Battalion, Canadian Infantry, when he was killed in action on 26 April 1917. He has no known grave but his name is commemorated on the Vimy Memorial in the Pas-de-Calais. His parents, William and Mary Baker, lived at St. Philipp's School House, Melville Road, Maidstone.

William Baldwin was 25 years of age and a private (874283) in 'B' Company of the 31st Battalion, Canadian Infantry, although he had initially enlisted with the 184th Battalion. He was killed in action on 3 May 1917 and his name is commemorated on the Vimy Memorial. His wife Maude was a native of Maidstone.

Sidney George Beadle was born in Maidstone. He enlisted in the Army two weeks after the outbreak of the war, on 19 August 1914 at Ponders End, having just turned 20 years of age. He became a private (754) with the 'D' 11th Battalion, Duke of Cambridge's Own (Middlesex Regiment). He first arrived in France on 31 May 1915 and was promoted while in theatre to the rank of lance corporal, along with being awarded the Military Medal for his bravery in the field. What he might have lacked in size – he was 5′ 3″ tall and weighed 8 stone 3 lbs – he certainly made up for with his grit and determination to get the job done. His Army service record shows that he spent time receiving medical treatment for an unspecified matter between 2 and 24 October 1915, during which time he visited a casualty clearing station, No 18 Field Ambulance and No 12 General Hospital at Rouen. He was wounded in action on 3 March 1916 and was admitted to military hospitals at both Rouen and Étaples, to be treated for gunshot wounds to his face and left forearm. He was killed in action on 11 April 1917 and is buried at the Happy Valley British Cemetery at Fampoux. Before he enlisted he worked as a gardener and was living at 7 Simpsons Road, Bromley, Kent, with his parents Percy and Hannah and his three brothers, Percy, Frederick and Bertie, along with two sisters, Maude and Phylis.

His elder brother, Percy Ernest Beadle, was a gunner (68023) in the Royal Garrison Artillery, having enlisted on 8 November 1915 at

Tottenham in North London. He saw service in France as part of the British Expeditionary Force between 1 and 12 June 1917, and then in Egypt between 27 September 1917 and 11 July 1919. He was finally demobilized on 12 September 1919. While in Egypt he became seriously ill with bronchopneumonia and at one stage there were concerns that he would not pull through as the telegram below, sent to his mother on 29 December 1918, shows:

> *Regret to inform you, officer commanding 69 General Hospital, Egyptian Expeditionary Force, reports your son No.68023, L/Bomb. P E Beadle, 123 Anti-Aircraft section, dangerously ill. Broncho Pneumonia.*

A week later they received another telegram dated 4 January 1919 informing them that Percy was now 'out of danger'. What a relief that must have been for all of his family.

Frederick Arthur Beadle also served during the war. He enlisted on 6 June 1916 at Tottenham having only just turned 18. He became Private 4225 with the 21st Battalion, Notts & Derbyshire Regiment, before being transferred to 'A' 17th Battalion, Gloucester Regiment, on 20 September 1917. He was disciplined once during his military service for having a dirty rifle on a company parade, for which his punishment was to be confined to barracks for three days. He survived the war and was finally demobilized on 11 October 1919.

Younger brother Bertie was too young to have served during the war, having not been born until 1905.

W. Gardner was 42 years of age and a gunner (156552) in 'C' Battery, 251st Brigade, Royal Field Artillery, when he was killed in action on 15 May 1917. He was buried at the London Cemetery in the village of Neuville-Vitasse. His widow Jessie lived at 22 Camden Street, Maidstone.

Charlie Gillespie Gates was 25 years of age and a corporal (19291) in the 6th Battalion, Queen's Own (Royal West Kent Regiment), when he was killed in action on 9 April 1917. He is buried at the Feuchy Chapel British Cemetery, at Wancourt. Before the war he worked as a clerk at a wholesale grocer's and on 5 December 1915 enlisted in the

Army becoming private 3926 in the 4/4th Battalion, Royal West Kent Regiment. He first arrived in France on 13 January 1917 and was promoted to the rank of lance corporal one month later. His parents, Frederick and Emma Gates, lived at 77 Holland Road, Maidstone, along with Charlie's three elder brothers, Harry, Horace and Ernest. Frederick and his wife Emma died within a few days of each other, Frederick on 13 January 1918 aged 64, and Emma on 25 January 1918 aged 59. One supposes this was due to the flu pandemic which spread throughout Europe at the time.

Horace Alfred Gates was a private in the 1st/1st Battalion, Kent Regiment, and saw service in Bombay.

Ernest Alfred Gates was born in Maidstone in 1886. He had married Daisy Flewitt on 4 July 1914 at Maidstone, exactly one month before the outbreak of the war. He had enlisted, aged 29, on 7 Dec 1915 when he was working as a cashier and living at 43 Campbell Road, Maidstone. He became a gunner (159846) in the Royal Garrison Artillery. He survived the war and passed away on 17 October 1957 aged 71, still living in Maidstone.

Stephen Medhurst was 25 years of age and a private (4168) in the 8th Battalion, Queen's Own (Royal West Kent Regiment), when he was killed in action on 11 April 1917. He is buried at the Maroc British Cemetery which is located in the French village of Grenay. His father Albert Medhurst, a widower, lived at 4 Thorner's Yard, Upper Stone Street, Maidstone.

Frank Mills was 33 years of age and a private (15593) in the 1st Battalion, Queen's Own (Royal West Kent Regiment), when he was killed in action on 10 April 1917. He is buried at the Bois-Carre British Cemetery, just outside the village of Thelus. He was a native of Maidstone, although his widow Phoebe lived at 'Rosemount', Wychling, Sittingbourne.

Sidney Thomas Obee was born in Maidstone in 1885. After the outbreak of the war he enlisted and became a private (47245) in the 22nd (Tyneside Scottish) Battalion, Northumberland Fusiliers. He was killed in action on 9 April 1917 and is buried at the Bailleul Road East Cemetery at Saint-Laurent-Blangy. His parents, Sidney and Minee Obee, lived at 90 Beresford Road, Gillingham.

Stephen Thomas Raggatt was 33 years of age and a gunner (93460) in the 213th Siege Battery, Royal Garrison Artillery, when he was killed in action on 28 April 1917. He is buried in the Henin Communal Cemetery Extension. His wife Clara Elizabeth lived at 9 Hope Street, Maidstone.

T.C. Steel was 29 years of age and a sergeant (9089) in the 1st Battalion, Bedfordshire Regiment, when he was killed in action on 23 April 1917. He is buried at the Lapugnoy Cemetery. He was a married man and lived with his wife at 5 Upper Fant Road, Maidstone.

Donald Reginald Vincent Starke lived with his parents Vincent and Emma Starke and his three sisters, Winnifred, Mabel, and Dorothy, at 28 Marsham Street, Maidstone. After the beginning of the war he enlisted as a rifleman (553174) in the 16th Battalion, London Regiment (Queen's Westminster Rifles). He had previously had the service number of 6683 while serving in the same battalion. He was killed in action on 17 April 1917 at 19 years of age and is buried at the Warlincourt Halte British Cemetery in the village of Saulty.

Herbert Beresford White was 21 years of age and a lieutenant in the 23rd Brigade, Royal Field Artillery, when he was killed in action on 13 April 1917. He is buried at the Chocques Military Cemetery in the Pas-de-Calais. His parents, Herbert and Beatrice White, had lived at The Poplars, 110 Tonbridge Road, Maidstone. Herbert was their only child.

William Levi Whitehead was 27 years of age and a private (357525) in 'C' Company, 2nd/10th Battalion, The King's (Liverpool Regiment), when he was killed in action on 14 April. He is buried at the Communal Cemetery Extension, which is located on the outskirts of the town of Estaires. His parents, William and Harriet Whitehead, lived at 19 St. John Street, Maidstone, with their other children, son Frederick and daughters Rose and Ivy.

It is clear to see from this how just one battle could have a profound and long lasting effect on a village, town or city, on their friends and relatives as well as the communities from which they came.

Two other Maidstone men were killed in France at this time. George Shorter Batcheller was 33 years of age and a gunner (115212) in the 225th Siege Battery, Royal Garrison Artillery, when he died of his wounds at the 44th Field Ambulance on 28 March 1917. He is buried at the Faubourg D'Amiens Cemetery in Arras. His death was announced in the *Sevenoaks Chronicle and Kentish Advertiser* on 20 April 1917. His parents, Robert and Julia Batcheller, lived at Highfield in Maidstone and his wife Minnie, who had been born in India, lived at 75 St. Luke's Road, Maidstone. Before the war George had his own business as a timber merchant. George and Minnie had lost a child in the first year of their marriage, possibly in childbirth.

Harold William Proctor had worked for the Maidstone branch of the London and Provincial Bank, prior to enlisting in the Army. He had initially enlisted as a private in the Queen's Own (Royal West Kent Regiment) before receiving a commission in the same regiment, with whose 6th Battalion he was serving at the time of his death. While leading his men in France on 9 April 1917 he was shot through the neck, and although urged to remain where he was and wait for a stretcher party, he refused to do so and carried on leading his men despite having to deal with heavy enemy fire. A short while later he received a fatal gunshot wound to the head and dropped dead. He was 27 years of age and is buried at the Feuchy Chapel British Cemetery in Wancourt in the Pas-de-Calais.

The empty cruelty of the war and the fact that it did not distinguish between the social classes was brought home in the strongest possible terms on 13 January 1917 with the news that the eldest son of the Mayor and Mayoress of Maidstone had been killed on New Year's Day. He was buried at the Heilly Station Cemetery at Méricourt-l'Abbé which is a village situated approximately ten miles north of Amiens. The following article appeared in the *Whitstable Times & Herne Bay Herald* of 13 January 1917:

Bereavement of the Mayor and Mayoress

News has been received of the death in action of Lieutenant Eric Clark, the eldest son of the Mayor and Mayoress of Maidstone, Councillor and Mrs G Foster Clark. The sad intelligence was conveyed to them on Thursday, in a War Office telegram, which read:- Deeply regret to inform you that Lieut. Eric Foster Clark, RFC, was killed in action January 1st. Army Council express their sympathy. – Secretary, War Office.

Lieutenant Eric Foster Clark was in fact attached to the Royal Fliyng Corps from The Buffs (East Kent Regiment). The 1911 census shows Eric as a boarder at the Mill Hill Public Secondary School in Hendon, London. In his will he left the sum of £2,101 8s 0d to his father the Mayor. The family home was at The Lodge, Boughton Mount, Boughton Monchelsea, near Maidstone. The Mayor lived there with his wife Henrietta and their daughters Mary and Joan, along with their son Hubert. There were also three servants who lived at the property. George Clark made his money as a manufacturer of grocer's sundries. Although Hubert would go on to become a professional musician, he too became a pilot, qualifying on 9 May 1939, just at the beginning of the Second World War. There was a younger son, Henry.

On Friday, 5 January 1917, the *Western Times* reported that Commander Noel Laurence DSO and bar was to be presented with the Freedom of Maidstone the next day. Noel Laurence had been born in Maidstone in 1882 and joined the Navy at the age of seventeen in 1899. Within five years he had been promoted to the rank of lieutenant and had become something of an expert in the fledgling world of submarines. He was the first officer of the British Royal Navy to take a submarine, the *E1*, into the Baltic Sea after the outbreak of the war, where he worked with the Russians. In 1915 the *E1* sank a German

HMS EI, Submarine.

transport ship and damaged the German Battle Cruiser the SMS *Moltke*. He was awarded the DSO for his work in the Baltic, along with the Russian awards of Order of St. George, 4th Class, and the Order of St. Vladimir, 4th Class with swords. He later served on the Royal Navy submarine *J1* when he torpedoed two German battleships near Jutland. He was awarded a bar to his DSO and was made a Chevalier of the Legion of Honour by the French.

His parents, Frederick and Fanny, lived at Somerfield Terrace, London Road, Maidstone.

His brother Roger died while serving with the Canadian Infantry in France on 9 April 1918. He was 39 years of age and also served in the 2nd Boer War of 1899-1902. He is buried at the Ecoivres Military Cemetery in Mont-Saint-Eloi in the Pas-de-Calais.

Another brother Malcolm also served with the Canadian forces, and another brother, Colin, was a flight sub-lieutenant in the Royal Naval Air Service.

Conscription had been introduced in the previous year and military tribunals were taking place most weeks in towns throughout Great Britain. Maidstone was no exception, with the West Kent Appeal Tribunals nearly always heard at Maidstone. The first one of the year was held at the town hall on Friday, 12 January 1917. The panel of those hearing the cases included Sir John Bromhead Matthews (chairman), Lord Amherst, and Mr Prosser (clerk). By the end of the evening all of those who had sat before the tribunal had gone home in differing states of happiness, free to carry on going about their daily business in the knowledge that they would not immediately have to rush off and adorn themselves in khaki.

The annual meeting of the Kent Farmers' Union took place at Maidstone Town Hall on Thursday, 1 February 1917. All of the delegates were welcomed by the Mayor of Maidstone, Mr George Foster Clark. He gave a rousing speech about the importance and need for every industry to combine its efforts and provide a collective representation of its individual interests, for its own benefit as well as that of the country as a whole, especially in a time of war. His words of encouragement and support came a month after his elder son Eric had become a casualty of the war. He went on say that he found it impressive and commendable in such difficult times, and with manpower for farmers at a premium, that they had managed to keep their union going, and that it was important that they did so.

Mr B. Champion, the chairman of the Kent branch of the National Farmers Union, thanked the mayor for his support and the use of Maidstone Town Hall for their meeting, his words echoed by all those present.

One of the first items on the agenda was to appoint a new chairman, as, having filled the position for two years, Mr Champion had decided not to seek re-election. In his closing address he spoke of how they should congratulate themselves that the union was in a much stronger position than it had been two years earlier. They were at a time in history when to ensure they were heading in the right direction was absolutely essential. It hadn't always been a smooth journey, especially since the beginning of the war. There were those who had accused them of profiteering from the war rather than seeing the sterling work they were doing for the good of the country. Hearing such unfair comments and unjust accusations had left a bad taste in the mouth. He spoke passionately about the benefits of being a member of the National Farmers Union and, although accepting that sometimes such a commitment was time consuming, it was extremely worthwhile. His hope was that one day not only would every farmer in Kent be a member of the union, but every farmer in the country.

The subscription each farmer paid was based on the acreage of their farm. They were asked to pay a halfpenny per acre of land that they farmed and the same again to cover administrative costs. The chairman added that if those in the union who were doing the job of bringing work to the farmers weren't earning them a halfpenny per acre of land, then they were doing no good. He contended however that the work being done was worth many shillings per acre, which even those farmers who chose not to subscribe to the union benefitted from as well. He was concerned by the fact that farmers were being mucked about by the government. One minute they were told that for every farm labourer who was needed to go off and fight in the war, they would be found a replacement, but suddenly that was no longer the case, and they simply had to make do with what they had, while still managing to deliver a rising level of productivity. The industry, he felt, was at a crossroads, teetering on a knife edge. He was concerned that the military did not understand their business, and this was not helped by the never-ending reel of red tape by which they were restrained. But he added that they had his utmost respect, facing death and destruction on a daily basis as they did. Mr Chapman had every confidence in his successor, who was a national farmer, already doing the work equally well, if not better than he himself had done. In closing he said that he desired to move a resolution for farmers to increase the country's production of corn and other similar crops, calling upon their deep-rooted patriotism to come to the fore and show the doubters how wrong and misguided they were in their views of them.

A letter had been sent in to the meeting by the Kent War Agricultural Committee requesting that the Kent branch of the National Farmers Union cooperate with them in arranging pigeon shoots for three consecutive weeks, because of the damage they were causing on some of the farms. They agreed to the request, and Wednesday afternoons were the preferred days to carry out the shoots.

On Saturday, 12 May 1917, Clifford Allen, who was the chairman of the Non-Conscription Fellowship, was released from Maidstone Prison after having served 112 days' imprisonment with hard labour. He had been court-martialled for refusing to obey military orders. This was the second time he had served a sentence for the same offence. On his release he was immediately handed over to a military escort to be returned to his unit. Despite his release, he was soon court-martialled yet again for the same offence.

The Non-Conscription Fellowship had been set up by Allen and fellow pacifist Fenner Brockway at the outbreak of the war. Theirs was an organisation that encouraged men to refuse to carry out war service and required its members to 'refuse from conscientious motives to bear arms because they consider human life to be sacred'. Both Allen and Brockway were arrested in late 1916 for handing out leaflets that criticized the government's introduction of compulsory conscription. They were put before the courts and fined, but when they refused to pay the fines, they were both sentenced to two months' imprisonment, which they served at Pentonville. On his release, Brockway was rearrested and for one night had the distinction of been held as a prisoner in the Tower of London.

On the afternoon of Saturday, 30 June 1917, a tragedy befell the people of Maidstone, not because of anything to do with the war, but just bad luck. Four children of the Page family from Ewel Manor Cottage, West Farleigh, were playing on the bank of the river Medway near Teston Bridge. The two younger children, Arthur and his sister Olive, fell into the water at a spot where the bank of the river drops away quite sharply. In the commotion the two elder children cried out for help. Their cries for help were heard by the son of a local farmer, David Bowerman, who was about 200 yards away. He ran to the river bank as quickly as he could and on his arrival found Olive struggling in the water close to the shore line, but Arthur had already been carried by the rapid current into midstream. David Bowerman, who was only 14 years of age himself, waded into the water, as did a wounded soldier from Barham Court who happened to be passing. Between them they managed to rescue Olive and bring her to the safety of the shore, but while they did so, Arthur had sadly disappeared from sight. The soldier was convalescing at the time at the nearby Barham Court Auxiliary Hospital at Teston, recovering from the effects of not one, but three wounds. But despite his injuries he carried Olive home to her family. Arthur's body was later recovered from the river.

It seemed rather a strange decision to make while the country was involved in a war which had no immediate end in sight, but a meeting took place on Thursday, 19 July 1917, at the Sessions House in Maidstone in relation to deciding on new electoral areas. Commissioners appointed under the Representation of the People Act held a meeting to hear any objections to the conclusions of the new parliamentary divisions of Kent. In essence the expected changes were that in future Kent would have a reduction in the number of MPs representing the people of the county, from fifteen to twelve. The new areas that would be covered were those of Canterbury, Dartford, Dover, Faversham, Gravesend, Isle of Thanet, Maidstone, North Western, Southern, and Tunbridge. This meant that the parliamentary areas of Chatham, Hythe and Rochester would completely disappear.

The following deaths were reported in the press on Friday, 10 August 1917, once again bringing the war directly to the homes of families in the Maidstone area:

Flight Commander Stephen Reginald Parke Walter of the Queen's (Royal West Surrey Regiment) and the Royal Flying Corps. He received his commission in December 1916 and was killed in action, aged 20, on 1 August 1917. He was the only child of Stephen, a retired captain in the 3rd Dragoon Guards, and Mrs Walter of The Parsonage, East Farleigh, Maidstone. At the time of his death he was attached to the 32nd Squadron, Royal Flying Corps. He is buried at the Lijssenthoek Military Cemetery which is situated in the West-Vlaanderen region of Belgium.

Frederick Mervyn Hills was the fourth son of Mr and Mrs Edward Hills of Lenworth, Maidstone. He was educated at Maidstone Grammar School as well as the Tonbridge School, where he played in both the

Lijssenthoek Military Cemetery (Permission CWGC).

schools' cricket and rugby teams. On completing his education, he began working in the field of civil engineering and found work in both America and Canada. He returned to the United Kingdom in 1914 for a holiday and at the outbreak of war became involved in the formation of the Public Schools Brigade for which he became the recruiting officer for the Maidstone district. Frederick received his commission in 1915 and first went out to France in 1916, but was returned home after contracting pneumonia. He went back to France in December 1916 and served in intelligence and as a lieutenant in charge of a Lewis gun crew. He was killed, along with five others, by a shell which hit his battalion headquarters on 27 July. His colonel wrote of him:

> *I have lost a very valuable officer, and one to whom we had all grown very attached while he was with us at Battalion Headquarters. He was beloved by his men, who have asked me to tell you how much they miss him, and how sorry they are for you.*

On 6 September 1917 an article appeared in the *Kent & Sussex Courier* about a theft. It concerned an Alice Winifred Malins, aged 30, who lived at 42 Bower Lane, Maidstone. She had recently been lodging at Beechwood Villas, Poundfield, where she had stolen the following unusual combination, a cup of tea, a slice of bread, syrup and suet pudding, which belonged to a Mrs Ellen Gerrish of Upton, Station Road, Crowborough, on 29 August. Ellen Knight, a maid who worked for Mrs Gerrish, told the court that on Wednesday, 29 August, there was a knock at the back door of the property at about eight o'clock in the morning. On opening the door she was confronted by Alice Malins who asked for a cup of tea and something to eat. When told that she would have to first ask her mistress, Malins pushed past Ellen Knight, went into the kitchen, and drank a cup of tea. She asked for some bread and butter, but when refused she cut herself a slice of bread and buttered it before rifling through a cupboard where she found some syrup. After spreading some onto the bread and butter, she quickly devoured it. She also took a piece of suet pudding which she started to eat as she left. Soon after leaving the house she was stopped in the High

Street by PC Wood who explained his suspicions and took her back to the home of Mrs Gerrish where she was identified by the maid. Despite this, Malins denied having stolen anything, but the magistrates did not believe her version of accounts and she was found guilty as charged. She was sent to prison for a month with hard labour. She had a previous conviction for soliciting and stealing a collection box.

The comments of Maidstone's Member of Parliament, Commander Bellairs, were widely reported in the press at the end of October 1917 in relation to questions he asked in the House of Commons in relation to promotion in the Navy. He asked whether the promotion of Sir Reginald Tyrwhitt, who had been uniformly successful, was to be delayed until over fifty captains senior to him had been promoted. In response to his question, Commander Bellairs received the following letter from Sir Reginald:

> *Dear Commander Bellairs,*
> *I should be grateful if in future you will refrain from taking a personal interest in my professional career. I am certainly content to leave my advancement in the hands of my superior officers, who have risen by merit to the positions they hold in the Admiralty.*

Commander Bellairs desired to offer Sir Reginald as full and as ample an apology as it was possible to give in regard to the personal aspect of the matter. His only reservation was that it was often not possible to talk in the House of Commons about promotion without citing individual cases.

On 24 November 1917 Mr Justice Bray, sitting at the Maidstone Assizes, was drawn to make a public speech before dealing with thirteen cases of bigamy, certainly an extremely high number:

> *Unfortunately the crime of bigamy is rampant at the present time. I am met with the difficulty that soldiers are wanted. Is a Judge to take in to consideration this fact, and either let them out or give them a small punishment in order that they may be free as soldiers to fight for their country?*

After careful consideration I have come to the conclusion that it is not a proper matter, as a rule, for a Judge to take this into consideration. The home Secretary can do so and does do so, and, in my opinion, the home Secretary is the proper person to deal with this matter. Necessarily, he has much more knowledge as to the grave urgency for soldiers than the Judge has.

It is always a difficult matter for a Judge to adjust the proper sentence to the particular case. The circumstances vary, and vary very greatly. The normal case I take to be a case where the wife has not been to blame, and where the woman has been deceived. Now before the war it was my practice, I think some Judges were not as severe, in those cases to give at least six months. Seeing this offence grow latterly I have given nine months. I think I must rise to twelve months, and therefore I am going to adjust my sentences upon that footing. The standard punishment is twelve months.

It is interesting that the numbers of bigamous marriages had risen so much. Maybe it was because the men concerned were going off to war and knew they might not be coming home.

Private James Scott Duckers was released from Maidstone Prison on 1 December 1917 by order of the Army Council; he decided to commute his last prison sentence. He was a conscientious objector who had been court-martialled on three occasions and had spent a total of nineteen months incarcerated in different civil and military prisons across the country. In 1921 he published a book entitled '*Handed-Over', The Prison Experiences of Mr J. Scott Duckers, Solicitor, of Chancery Lane, Under the Military Services Act*, which was his own story about those dark days in prison.

Since conscription, the issue of conscientious objectors had been a regular topic of discussion. On Tuesday, 4 December 1917, an article appeared in the *Evening Despatch* on that topic. Canon J.W. Horsley from Maidstone and the Rev. E.W. Barnes, Master of the Temple, both members of the Church of England Peace League, were concerned about the treatment of conscientious objectors, so much so that they sent high-ranking members of the church their views in the hope that they would support them in their efforts to bring the issue to the government's attention. What they had to say was short and to the point:

> *We, the undersigned members of the Church of England, would represent to the Government that great offence is being given to reason and conscience by the treatment, and especially in the repeated sentences and punishments, of some of those who from sincere conviction feel bound to refuse military service.*

A large number of bishops, deans, priests, and a number of laymen had all offered their written support to the letter.

CHAPTER 6

1918
The Final Blow

1918 was a year that would start with no end in sight, yet one which would ultimately see the end of the war and the signing of the Armistice. According to figures produced by the Commonwealth War Graves Commission website, during those final ten months, one week and four days of the war, 268,245 British and Commonwealth troops lost their lives. Three years later, by the end of 1921, that figure had risen by another 78,000 to 346,378 as men died from their wounds or from sickness.

With the end of the war in sight, the population of Maidstone, which numbered some 35,477, was fast approaching the dawning of a new post-war age.

On the home front the year began with allegations that Kent farmers were 'holding up' their cattle and preventing them from going to market on time, hence forcing up the price of beef in the shops. This didn't sit well with the farmers, as in essence it meant that they were being accused of profiteering from the war. The National Farmers Union of Kent held a meeting in Maidstone on 3 January 1918, as a result of which the Union's Secretary, Mr John Watson, wrote a letter to the editor of the *Dover Express* putting the Union's case:

MAIDSTONE'S WAR CROSS.

The Bishop of Croydon at the dedication of a very handsome churchyard

Maidstone War Cross.

Dear Sir,

The National Farmers Union of Kent desire in the most emphatic manner possible to protest against the untrue statements appearing in the Press that farmers are 'holding up' their cattle. This statement is a serious accusation against farmers, and one which our Prime Minister would not endorse, as he gives farmers credit for being as patriotic as any other class. The Press, almost since the commencement of the war have raised a tirade against farmers who have been doing and are doing, their utmost under most trying circumstances to raise the necessary foodstuffs for the people. There is little fear of farmers 'holding up' their cattle at present, they are only *too pleased to get quit of them whenever they are even partially fatted. Admittedly there is a shortage of meat, but who has brought about this unfortunate situation? Practical farmers have pointed out again and again to the Food Controller what would be the result of this policy, and it has come to pass.*

Had production been encouraged, we had an abundance of store cattle and an abundance of roots, but Lord Rhondda's proposal was an economic one, therefore, it failed. He has now raised his price for beef, but this cannot be produced in five minutes, it takes months.

Is it better to have meat at a nominally dear price, or a dearth of meat at a controlled price? The Food Controller is again courting disaster on the milk question; his proposition is to give milk producers this coming summer 3d per gallon less than they had last summer, despite the fact that milk cows have advanced in price enormously and labour is more difficult to obtain.

This policy will again fail, and we consider it our duty to point this out to the Food Controller, as to be without milk will be even more serious than a temporary shortage of milk.

Lord Rhondda was the Minister of Food Control in the latter years of the war. He had made his fortune as the owner of the Cambrian Collieries. In May 1915 he was on board the RMS *Lusitania* with his daughter Margaret when it was torpedoed by a German submarine. They both survived. He was recognized as being successful in introducing an efficient system of rationing during the First World War. He died on 3 July 1918.

A remarkable encounter took place at the Maidstone Borough Tribunal at the Sessions House in Maidstone on Monday, 25 February 1918, between Mr Robert Vaughan Gower, the Mayor of Tunbridge Wells, and Mr Brennan, the legal representative of a man who was appearing before the tribunal on the grounds that he was suffering from valvular disease of the heart. It was Mr Vaughan Gower's first time at one of the tribunals as a national service representative. On hearing the grounds of the appeal Mr Vaughan Gower remarked that the man concerned could undergo a medical re-examination to determine if his condition had worsened or improved. This led to the following spat:

Mr Brennan: Mr Vaughan Gower, you are a rejected man yourself, and I ask you to please show your sympathy with the unfit.

Mr Vaughan Gower (to the chairman): It is most improper that an advocate should come here and make such remarks.

Mr Brennan: Don't lecture me Mr Vaughan Gower. We are not going to submit to your impertinence. The methods that prevail at Tunbridge Wells will not be tolerated here.

The Chairman: I don't want to take up a strong line with regard to the matter, but I must ask Mr Brennan to behave himself as an advocate in performing his duties here.

Mr Brennan: I was improperly attacked Mr Vaughan Gower when I reminded you that the Army was no place for a young man suffering from valvular disease of the heart.

The Chairman: This is Mr Vaughan Gower's first appearance here. We have a lot of business to get through, and I am sure the course taken will not help us to facilitate matters. Both Mr Vaughan Gower and we as a Tribunal have a public duty to perform, and we want to work amicably together.

Mr Brennan: But, Mr Chairman, I am not going to have my remarks attacked in the way Mr Vaughan Gower attacked them. My client suffers from a physical disability which should entitle him to the sympathy of others in the same position.

Sadly, the report didn't outline how the conversation continued and what the outcome and findings of the tribunal were. Valvular heart disease is rare in the under-50s.

The *Whitstable Times and Herne Bay Herald* dated Saturday, 2 March 1918, included a report concerning air raids and street lighting. To obviate the necessity of cutting off the town's general electricity supply as a precaution during an enemy air raid, the Maidstone authorities took the decision that no street lights would be lit for seven days before and seven days after a full moon, other than those that had been served by a special cable in the High Street, Week Street, and the lower part of Tonbridge Road. These were controlled by a central switch and it was possible for them to be switched off without interfering with the electricity supply to homes, factories and businesses. Warnings of air raids were indicated to households by lowering the brightness of their lights three times, but without cutting off the electrical supply. After an air raid was over, the 'all clear' signal was given in a similar manner. The reign of Queen Victoria had come to an end with her death on 22 January 1901, and although there had been technological breakthroughs in the field of electricity during her reign, it was still somewhat in its infancy. Electricity was available throughout the war years, but the use of candles and oil burners was still widespread.

Maidstone Zeppelins poster.

On Friday 29 March 1918, the funeral took place of 28-year-old Lieutenant Arthur William Edmett at Maidstone cemetery. He was wounded in action while serving in France with the 10th Battalion, Queen's Own (Royal West Kent Regiment), on 22 September 1917. He died of his wounds at Guys Hospital in London on Saturday, 16 March. A service was held in his memory at King Street Church in Maidstone.

His younger brother Eric Geoffrey Edmett, who was a private (24/1650) in the 1st Battalion, Auckland Regiment, New Zealand Expeditionary Force, was killed in action on 7 June 1917 aged 21. He has no known grave but his name is commemorated on the Messines Ridge New Zealand Memorial which is situated in the West-Vlaanderen region. Their mother Fanny lived at The Elms, Maidstone.

A letter dated 4 April 1918 appeared in the *Sevenoaks Chronicle and Kentish Advertiser* on 12 April 1918, sent in by Lieutenant Colonel J.P. Dalison, Commanding Officer, Depot, Royal West Kent Regiment. He was also the chairman of the Regimental Care Committee of the West Kent Prisoners of War Committee which was located at the barracks in Maidstone. It was about British soldiers from the West Kent area who were being held as prisoners of war in German camps and their treatment. The sender was concerned that not enough people from the West Kent area were aware of the plight of the prisoners of war. It was hoped that the more people who knew, the more would be prepared to help as well as provide food items and money.

The number of British soldiers from the West Kent area who were being held as prisoners of war ran into the hundreds and the cost of sending them food was somewhere in the region of two thousand pounds each month. Because of food shortages in Germany, which affected both the civilian population as well as the military, feeding British prisoners of war wasn't high on their list of priorities. There were concerns that the food parcels that were being sent to captured British soldiers were not getting through to them, but instead were being pilfered by their German guards, who were themselves starving.

Whatever was received by the committee at the barracks was forwarded on to the headquarters of the Central Prisoners of War Committee at 4 Thurloe Place in London, packed into food and clothes

British PoWs in Germany.

parcels, and despatched on to the men who were being held in Germany.

Each prisoner of war from the West Kent area, which included those from Maidstone, was sent six parcels every month during their captivity, and once every six months they were sent a complete outfit of clothes as well as a pair of serviceable boots. Each parcel that was sent out cost 8 shillings. In addition each man was sent 26lbs of bread from Switzerland on a monthly basis at a cost of 7s 6d per prisoner. At first the Association of Men of Kent and Kentish Men raised funds for prisoners of war, but in March 1915 the War Office sanctioned the appointment of the Prisoners of War Help Committee, a voluntary organisation. In essence they oversaw the organisation and distribution of food parcels to all British PoWs and paid the costs.

To help with the cost of the parcels, members of the public in Maidstone and other towns throughout West Kent were encouraged to engage in a scheme of adopting a prisoner by either providing the content of the parcel or paying for its cost. The recipient of the parcel would then be informed of the name and address of the person who had paid for the parcel that had been sent to them.

As well as individuals, groups of people from parish churches, banks, businesses, and schools were also encouraged to get involved in the scheme.

On Wednesday, 15 May 1918, the Lord Lieutenant of Kent, John Charles Pratt, 4th Marquess Camden, presented Kentish men and women with their OBE medals. The presentation took place in the square opposite the Town Hall in Maidstone. The awards were for work and devotion to duty while involved in dangerous wartime incidents.

4th Marquess Camden.

One of the awards was presented to Miss Mabel Lethbridge. This is how it was reported on page 2 of the *Daily Mirror* on Saturday, 18 May 1918:

OBE Medal for Kent heroine

One of the recipients of an OBE medal at Maidstone yesterday was Miss Mabel Lethbridge, who was awarded the decoration for a conspicuous act of bravery in a munitions factory as a result of which she lost one leg and sustained injuries to the other.

The article did not include the name or location of the munitions factory, in keeping with the directives of the Defence of the Realm Act 1914. Here is the full story:

Mabel Lethbridge wasn't from Maidstone and as far as I know she had no connection with the town other than that was where she received her OBE, but I still feel her story is worth telling. She was born in Luccombe on 7 July 1900. In 1917, when not quite 17 years of age, she became a nurse at Bradford Hospital where she cared for wounded

British soldiers who had been sent home from the Western Front. By October the same year she had moved to London and, having lied about her age, she took up a position working at the National Munitions Filling Factory in Hayes Middlesex where she filled artillery shells with Amatol explosive. On 23 October she was working on a machine that packed the Amatol into the shells. The particular machine that Mabel was working on had already been condemned by the factory authorities, but because of the government's continuing demand for more and more shells she was told to carry on using it. There was an explosion which killed several of her colleagues, blew one of her legs off and

Mabel Florence Lethbridge.

damaged the other. She was also temporarily blinded. Luckily for her she managed to stay conscious, realise the seriousness of her situation and apply a tourniquet to her thigh, which undoubtedly saved her life. Even though she was awarded the OBE, the government held back from awarding her a disability pension because when she had started working at the factory she had lied about her age to get the job. Through today's eyes, it does appear a very strange and unjust decision.

After the war she became a writer, penning three volumes of her autobiography, she married, had a child, divorced, remarried and became an estate agent. Her efforts made her wealthy enough to own and maintain a house in London as well as a rural residence in Chertsey. During the Second World War she worked for the Ambulance Service throughout the Blitz on London.

According to the 1911 census, Miss Maude Agnes Victoria Nichols was born on 11 February 1897 in Maidstone and lived at Lindenhurst, Buckland Road, Maidstone, with her mother Kate, her sister, also Kate, her three brothers, William, James and Robert, and Myrtle Jane Leppingwell, who was the family's servant. The following article appeared in the *Kent & Sussex Courier* of Friday, 21 June 1918:

Captain Claude Templer, who after thirteen unsuccessful attempts, escaped from Germany and re-joined his regiment in France, has now been killed in action, aged twenty-two. He only received his Captaincy in May, and a pathetic incident is that his engagement to Miss Maude Nichols, of Maidstone, was to have been announced shortly.

Captain Claude Lethbridge Templer was killed in action on 4 June 1918 while serving with the 1st Battalion, Gloucestershire Regiment. His body was never recovered, he has no known grave and his name is commemorated on the Loos Memorial which is situated in the Pas-de-Calais region of France. He was captured by the Germans on 22 December 1914 near Givenchy while reconnoitring enemy positions. In captivity he continually made efforts to escape, thirteen in total, before he was eventually successful in 1917. So impressed was the King with Templer's exploits that he granted him a private audience. Other than that, he received no official recognition for his acts of derring-do. In 1918 he returned to the Western Front where he was killed in action, after returning from a successful raid on a German trench. His engagement to Maude sadly never took place and she was left to mourn her painful loss as best she could. She did eventually find happiness when in August 1922 she married Louis C.A. Smith who I believe also served during the First World War.

The British Army Pension Records which cover the period of the First World War show a Louis Charles Anthony Smith who enlisted as a private (495251) in the 2nd/2nd Home Counties Field Ambulance, Royal Army Medical Corps on 24 November 1914 when he was 21 years of age. The same record also shows that on 28 June 1915 he was promoted from lance corporal to quartermaster sergeant. Very impressive. He arrived in France on 25 January 1917 and served at both the 12th and 66th Casualty Clearing Stations. On 7 April he inhaled a small dose of poison gas. The next day he reported feeling unwell and was suffering with a cough, chest pains, headache, a sore throat, his pulse was slow and he had marked anaemia. On 17 April he was sent back to England on board the hospital ship *Carisbrook Star*. After some extensive treatment at the 2nd/1st Southern General Hospital in Dudley Road, Birmingham, he was discharged from the Army on 22 October 1918 as being no longer physically fit for wartime military service. I believe that this is the same Louis C.A. Smith who Maude Nichols married in 1922.

An outbreak of the Spanish influenza pandemic that was sweeping across large swathes of the world hit Maidstone with a vengance in July 1918. What was described in the local press at the time as 'an important factory in Maidstone' had nearly eighty members of staff who failed to turn up for work because of the flu. The factory referred to is more than likely to have been a munitions factory, but because of wartime reporting restrictions brought in as part of the Defence of the Realm Act 1914, the naming of the factory and what it produced were restricted. At the same factory, other workers started reporting sick throughout the course of the day and were immediately sent home and told to remain there.

An article appeared in the *Kent & Sussex Courier* on 5 July 1918 concerning the subject of war pensions and training opportunities for certain categories of wounded soldiers which made for interesting reading. The article was written by Mr F.G. Stenning who lived at 50 Earl Street, Maidstone. The government, through the Ministry of War Pensions, made extensive arrangements for the training of soldiers who had been discharged from the Army on medical grounds and because of their injuries were unable to return to their pre-war employment or to resume them to the same degree as they had previously. The list of the available training opportunities included the following:

Fruit basket making – the course was taking place at Langley near Maidstone and there were vacancies for only three men. Although today basket making might appear to seem nothing more than a hobby, back in 1918 the county of Kent was awash with orchards of all different types of fruits and baskets were big business. At harvest time the fruit was collected in wicker baskets which meant a continuous need for more and more of them. Most of the osier baskets that were used in Kent's orchards before the outbreak of hostilities were imported from Belgium and, with the war, the source of the baskets was no more. Shortage followed, and that meant the need for men to be trained in making them in England. The training to be a fruit basket maker remarkably took six months to complete, after which time the trainer on the course would provide those who had reached an acceptable standard with paid work at the standard piece work rate of pay. The main stipulation for the work was the use of both hands and feet, which immediately prevented 250,000 from applying for the course. The same training was also available on a course at nearby Otford, where six places were available.

Boot repairing – this proved to be extremely popular, with the courses being filled nearly as quickly as they were made available. Training was also being offered with private employers but most of these opportunities were in Surrey and London and not in the Maidstone area.

Commercial subjects – in the main this meant office clerks and was available at the Technical Institute in Maidstone, although each course required ten applicants to sign up for it before it could commence.

Cricket ball making – this wouldn't necessarily be the first type of employment many people would think about as a way of making a living, but it was a training opportunity that was being offered by the government. It required good eyesight and men who were quick with their fingers. The training course for this was at the cricket ball making factory in Tonbridge.

Brush making – this was one of the many industries which had made its home in Maidstone, including the Kent Brush Company factory. There were vacancies for several men to work and be trained in-house at the Maidstone factory.

Fruit Farming – this was a strenuous job and therefore not for the faint-hearted. A man needed to be fairly strong to undertake this type of job and be willing and able to work on the land in all types of weather conditions, come rain or shine. It involved the moving of heavy ladders, digging and cultivation of the land and orchards.

Furniture – Back in the middle of 1918, there were no vacancies in the Maidstone area for those wounded soldiers who saw being a furniture maker, French polisher or upholsterer as their future way of earning a living, but the Ministry of Pensions was keen for firms and businesses involved in the manufacture of furniture to become involved in their scheme.

Electrical engineers – these were going to be in demand in post-war Britain, and with a readily available source of manpower who had spent their war serving with the Royal Engineers, finding enough suitable applicants was not a problem. The training course was six months long, but it was worth it as everybody who passed the course was subsequently found full-time employment in the industry. Some of the courses were held at Maidstone's Technical Institute.

It was refreshing to see the British government of the day actively participating, in the form of the Ministry of Pensions, in doing all they could to help wounded soldiers.

The *Whitby Gazette* carried an article on 12 July 1918 concerning what was described as a farcical prosecution by officers from Maidstone police. The circumstances of the incident were as follows. A cyclist was summonsed by magistrates at Maidstone for riding a cycle without a light. In the evidence given by the officer concerned, it came out that the defendant had been chatting with a neighbour of his who lived only a few doors away from him. While talking to each other, the lighting up hour had arrived, meaning that any cycles or other vehicles on the road had to display their lights. Having finished his conversation with his neighbour, and without thinking, the defendant climbed onto his cycle and rode back to his own home without displaying a light. A constable, who had been watching the two men in conversation, decided to measure the distance between the two properties and on doing so discovered that it was 122 and a half yards. That the officer decided to report the matter is hard enough to understand, but why the officer's sergeant then agreed to send the matter before the local magistrates is even more so. The magistrates dismissed the summons on payment by the defendant of costs. It is hard to believe that in the circumstances of the time the police would not have had more important issues to deal with!

It was confirmed on Wednesday, 17 July, that Royal Air Force 1st Class Air Mechanic Sergeant 39534 Stanley Robert Richmond had died on 10 May 1918. He was 23 years of age and was a member of 27 Squadron. Stanley was an observer and gunner on an aircraft which took part in a raid on German lines in France on 10 May 1918, during which his aircraft was shot down. It was at first hoped that Stanley and his pilot had survived and been taken prisoner by the Germans, but the Red Cross in Geneva informed the British authorities that the Germans had reported that both the pilot and the observer were killed in the crash. Stanley was buried at the Caix British Cemetery in the Somme. Three other members of 27 Squadron are shown as having been killed on the same day as Stanley and are buried in the same cemetery: Second Lieutenant Lawrence Edwin Dunnett, Lieutenant Arthur Haddon Hill and Second Lieutenant D H Prosser. Which of the three was the pilot of the aircraft that Stanley was an observer in is not known. He was the eldest son of George and Miriam Richmond of 22 Muir Road, Maidstone. Stanley had previously served as a driver with the Army Service Corps, with whom he had enlisted two months shy of his twentieth birthday on 15 September 1914 at Maidstone. His service number was T4/238823, indicating that the unit was part of the Territorial Force, which in turn was part of the Kent Brigade Reserve Company, Army Service Corps. On enlisting, he voluntarily agreed to serve overseas if so required, even though there was no compulsion for him to do so. He was discharged on 26 July 1916 when he transferred to the Royal Flying Corps.

The people of Maidstone received the news on 18 August 1918 that one of their oldest residents had sadly passed away. William Fancett was 103 years of age, having been born in East Fairleigh, Kent, in May

1815, six weeks before the Battle of Waterloo. At the time of his death he was living at 36 Brewer Street, Maidstone, with Susan Bezant, who was 84 years of age, and her niece Rose Doe. Other than failing eyesight, he still remained in possession of all of his faculties. His wife Mary had died sometime after 1871. There were two children from the marriage, Sarah, who was born in 1846, and John, who was born in 1850. Sarah died in 1907 but, according to the 1911 census, John, who by then was 61 years of age, was still alive and living at 28 Whitmore Street, Maidstone.

William Fancett was also the last surviving member of the committee which worked for Benjamin Disraeli during his candidature to become the Member of Parliament for Maidstone in 1837. Up until this time, he had spelt his name D'Israeli, but before his election address that year was printed in the *Maidstone and Kentish Journal*, which he had personally dictated in front of the newspaper's editor, and just before the writer was about to add his signature to it, he turned to him and said, 'Omit the apostrophe: It gives the name a foreign appearance; and write it in one word, Disraeli.' Hence it appeared for the first time in the form in which it has been written ever since.

After the declaration of the poll he wrote the briefest of letters to his sister informing her of the result:

> *Maidstone*
> *July 27, 1837, 11 O'clock*
> *Dearest,*
>   *Lewis*   *707*
>   *Disraeli*   *616*
>   *Colonel Thompson*   *412*
> *The constituency nearly exhausted.*
>
> *In haste*
> *Dizzy.*

Although the letter shows Disraeli finished in second place, Maidstone actually had two parliamentary seats and he was duly elected. The man who beat Disraeli, Wyndham Lewis, was, like

Disraeli, a Conservative, who had also helped finance Disraeli's election campaign. Although there were less than 1,800 votes cast, this was not a reflection of the town's population, but more a case of the small minority of men who were eligible to vote at the time.

On Saturday, 24 August 1918, several Maidstone shop keepers were summonsed to appear before the local justice of the peace for supplying the Mons Star, service chevrons, and wound stripes to persons not authorized to wear them.

Wound stripe.

The proceedings were brought by the local police, and it was explained that under the Defence of the Realm Regulations it was an offence to supply these articles, or military uniforms, without lawful authority, and that tradesmen should first satisfy themselves that the purchasers were entitled to wear such items. The solicitor who was collectively defending the group of shop keepers said that as far as they were all aware there was nothing to prevent the free sale of these articles. He also pointed out that there was nothing to prevent the military authorities from regulating the matter by simply prohibiting the sales, by ensuring that anybody trying to purchase such items could only do so on production of an official permit or licence. The bench considered the case to be proven and that all of the defendants were guilty as charged, but dismissed them under the Probation of Offenders Act, having regard to the fact that military uniforms, which come under the same regulations, were being sold by tradesmen all over the country without any action being taken against them by the War Office. For a man to wear a wound badge who hadn't actually been wounded in the war would have been considered an offensive act by anybody.

The *Chester Chronicle* dated Saturday, 31 August 1918, included an article about a wounded war hero. It told the story of the son of a Mr and Mrs T. Harding who had received a letter from an Army chaplain in France to say that their son Fred had courageously offered to provide some of his own blood to save the life of a wounded officer. The blood transfusion went ahead and the officer's life was saved. In his letter the chaplain wrote, 'He is a brave lad, and you are to be congratulated on having such a gallant son.' Private Harding, who had been wounded himself, was convalescing at Hayle Place Hospital in Maidstone and had subsequently written home to his parents as well.

Monday, 23 September 1918, saw the death of George Ernest Fowler a 33-year-old married man from East Malling at the Red Cross Racecourse Hospital Prestbury, Cheltenham, Gloucestershire. The hospital, which had opened on 28 October 1914, was actually housed in the grandstand.

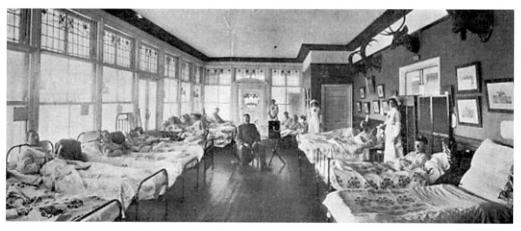

Racecourse VAD Hospital Cheltenham.

George had first arrived in France on 28 July 1915 as a private (21147) with the Grenadier Guards, before transferring to the Guards Machine Gun Regiment as Private 118. He had been severely wounded while serving in France and admitted to the Racecourse hospital on 6 September 1918. Both of his legs had been amputated before he died.

He was buried in the East Malling Churchyard. He left a wife, Elizabeth, and three young children, George, Robert and Elizabeth.

Tuesday, 1 October 1918, saw the death at the age of 71 of Viscount Falmouth at Mereworth Castle near Maidstone. The late viscount, Edward Thomas Boscawen, was the seventh holder of the title, having succeeded to it on the death of his father in 1889. His father, the sixth viscount, acquired Mereworth Castle when he married Baroness Le Despencer and there he bred many of Britain's top race horses of the day. The seventh viscount had joined the Coldstream Guards in 1866 as a lieutenant. By the time he retired in 1902, having served for thirty-six years, he had reached the rank of assistant military secretary to the commander-in-chief in Ireland. At the viscount's funeral, the King was represented by Colonel Sir Douglas Dawson and Queen Alexandra was represented by Lieutenant-Colonel F. Hardy.

Falmouth had lost two sons to the war. The Hon. Vere Douglas Boscawen had been a second lieutenant in the 1st Battalion, Coldstream Guards, and was 24 years of age when he was killed in action, early on in the war, on 29 October 1914. He has no known grave and his name is commemorated on the Ypres (Menin Gate) Memorial. The Hon. George Edward Boscawen was 29 and a major in the 116th Battery, Royal Field Artillery, when he died on 7 June 1918. He was a holder of the Distinguished Service Order. He is buried at the La Ville-aux-Bois British Cemetery which is situated in the Aisne region of France. There were also two of Falmouth's sons who survived the war, the Hon. Evelyn who served with the RAF and the Hon. Thomas who served with the Rifle Brigade.

Thursday, 3 October 1918, saw the death of Royal Air Force Cadet Bertram Leney from Maidstone at the Streatham Hall Military Hospital in Exeter. He had undergone a serious operation two weeks earlier which subsequently led to him dying of peritonitis. He was very popular with his fellow cadets and instructors for his ability as a pilot, his sense of humour and his athletic prowess, having represented the cadets at rugby. He was a splendid forward who had represented his native county of Kent on numerous occasions. He had also represented Blackheath, whose captain at the time was Captain W.S.D. Craven. Before the war Bertram had been a secretary to a brewery company.

He married Emily Gladys Baxter on 25 June 1912 at All Saints Parish Church in Marylebone, London. At the time of his death, Leney was 30 years of age, a married man, and living at Orpines in Wateringbury, Kent. He was also wealthy, having left a sum of £23,953 18s 3d in his will, which today would have an equivalent value of £1.25 million. The money was not left to his wife but to a Mr James Frederick Baxter. How he had amassed such a fortune is not known. Although at the time of his death he was training to be a pilot with the RAF, his actual regiment was the Royal Horse Artillery and Royal Field Artillery, with whom he held the rank of gunner (246086). He had previously been an acting lance corporal with the Inns of Court Officer Training Corps. The Commonwealth War Graves Commission website shows the date of Bertram's death as 30 October 1918. I am assuming that this is nothing more than a typo as all other documents record the date of his death as having been 3 October. He is buried in the Churchyard of the All Saints Parish Church, in West Farleigh in Kent.

Friday, 25 October 1918, saw the sitting of the West Kent Appeals Tribunal at the Sessions House in Maidstone. Although held in Maidstone, the tribunals heard appeals from men who lived in different parts of West Kent. The appeals panel included Mr Rowland Allen who was the chairman, with panel members Mr J. Barker, Mr C. Tuff, and Mr A.W. Tapp. Mr W.B. Prosser was the clerk and Lieutenant Colonel J.M. Rogers was the military representative.

The first case before them was that of Mr George William Savage, a 32-year-old married baker from Tunbridge Wells. He was granted a six-month exemption from having to enlist. In total the tribunal had nine cases before them, all of which were awarded certificates of exemption, ranging from two to six months. They included brewery workers, a dairy farmer, a plumber, an engineer and a malt grinder. The certificates given to each of the men meant that the war would be over before their exemptions had expired.

The same day saw the arrest of Mr John Ranger of 91 Holland Road, Maidstone, on suspicion of theft. Mr Ranger, a local taxation officer, was arrested at Maidstone railway station by Detective Constable Clow. He took Mr Ranger back to his home at 91 Holland Road where he was handed a revolver and a pair of gloves, both items that belonged to a Mr W.F. Palmer of the Market Hotel in Ashford. So seriously was the offence viewed that when Mr Ranger appeared at Ashford Police Court on Friday, 25 October, Mr C. Iggleston JP deemed it necessary to remand him in custody. When the case was reconvened on Monday, 28 October, Mr Palmer, the owner of the stolen items, told the court that on Wednesday, 23 October, when going down to the breakfast room in his hotel, he noticed that his overcoat had been moved. On closer examination he discovered that both his gun and gloves were missing. The newspaper article which reported the matter did not explain why Mr Ranger had stolen the items but, maybe more importantly, there was no reason given as to why Mr Palmer had a revolver in the first place and had left it in the pocket of his overcoat. Mr Ranger was remanded until the following day, but as he left the dock to be taken to the cells he had some kind of fit and had to be carried the rest of the way. He was deemed to have recovered sufficiently the following day to be brought back to court, where he faced further charges of theft. It was alleged that he had also stolen property belonging to Kent County Council, comprising capes and tins of paint. Evidence was presented to the court that the items went missing from the Sessions House in Maidstone. They were subsequently discovered at Mr Ranger's home. A third charge of theft came in the form of an allegation made by Mr Harold Bergerson, the landlord of the Kent Arms public house in Ashford, who stated that he had a quantity of shotgun cartridges stolen from the smoking room of his property, which were found at Ranger's home. Mr Flower, who represented Mr Ranger, suggested that his client 'was suffering from an unbalanced mind'. I have been unable to find how this case concluded.

Wednesday, 13 November 1918, just two days after the signing of the Armistice, saw a case brought before Judge Parry at Maidstone County Court which showed the existence of the parallel world which ran side by side with the horror and carnage of the war. While men had been dying on the battlefields of France and Belgium, Judge Parry had to deal with a man's right to pick and then sell the apples from the overhanging branches of his neighbour's apple tree, some of which encroached in to his garden. Judge Parry said that the defendant (the newspaper article had decided not to name either of the men involved) based his right to pick the apples on his right to lop overhanging branches on which apples grew. His right to lop the aforementioned branches could not be contested, assuming that it was done in a reasonable manner. The judge declared his view that, although a man might remove a nuisance, he could not in general appropriate the material that caused the nuisance. He awarded the plaintiff ten pounds in damages.

Death didn't leave Maidstone once the war was over. The ravages of the flu pandemic that was sweeping far and wide across Europe saw to that. In the week commencing 18 November 1918, Maidstone lost thirty-four of its citizens, including a mother and her three young children. It was the highest number of burials in the town in one day since the typhoid epidemic which had swept through the town in 1897.

On Friday 15 November 1918, four days after the signing of the Armistice, it was announced that the Ministry of Pensions was taking steps to see that the addition of 6s 6d to the flat rate payable to the childless wife was effectively administered and that this additional amount was payable as from Thursday, 1 November. These additional payments were paid as a matter of course in every case where a childless wife was unable to work, was unaccustomed to work, or was unable to obtain work without having to change where she lived. Those clear instructions made sure that any inequalities in administration amongst the different local war pension committees would no longer exist. The new rules meant that all childless wives were eligible for an allowance of up to 12 shillings a week to cover such things as hire-purchase payments and mortgage interest and insurance premiums if they could show that their present income was less than her income before her husband's enlistment after having taken into account the saving in expenditure which came about as a result of his absence. The regulations had not been widely advertised by the Ministry of Pensions, despite the support of the government and the good people of the nation who wanted to stand by the dependants of those who had borne the strain of the fighting on the battlefields of France, Belgium and beyond. The additional cost of paying the 6s 6d to the women who qualified for it was estimated to have cost the British government somewhere in the region of half a million pounds. There was also an increase in the grants paid to the dependants of soldiers and sailors who were unable to work. The War Pensions Committee were empowered to make grants in such cases of up to 50 per cent from 33 per cent of the assessed dependence.

Whatever the reason was behind the government's decision in making these additional payments, they were greatly appreciated by the recipients.

At long last the war was over. Four and a half years of bloody conflict had finally come to an end, leaving a mixture of relief and mourning. Everybody had been involved in the war and affected by it in some way or another; there weren't many families who hadn't experienced some kind of suffering, or the loss of a loved one.

CHAPTER 7

Maidstone's Famous

I felt that it would be interesting to take a look at some of the people who were either born or lived in Maidstone and who were alive during the years of the First World War, if for no other reason than to show the diversity of achievements of Maidstonians.

Robert Hughes 'Bobby' Beale was born in Maidstone on 8 January 1884. He had two elder brothers, Randall and Alfred, who like him were the sons of Walter and Esther Beale, but sadly Esther died in 1894 at 37 years of age. After Esther's death, Walter suddenly found himself with three young children to bring up while at the same time trying to maintain his furniture business. He married Lucy Teale in August 1895, with whom he went on to have a further six children. Robert Hughes Beale was a professional footballer.

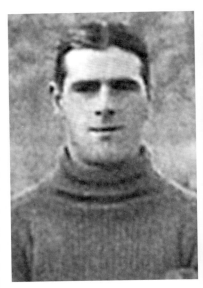

Robert Hughes Beale.

The first team he played for was Maidstone United, but he left them in 1905 when he joined the then Southern League outfit, Brighton & Hove Albion, where he played for three years. In 1908 he moved on to Norwich City, who were then also playing in the Southern League, by which time Norwich had only been in existence for six years. In May

1912 he was transferred to Manchester United for the sum of £275 (the equivalent of £28,000 today). He made his debut on 2 September 1912 in a 0-0 draw against Arsenal, and went on to play a total of 105 matches for the Red Devils. He also represented the English League against the Scottish League during the 1912-13 season, as well as taking part in trial matches for the North against the South of England. The war put a stop to the English domestic league during the 1914-15 season and it didn't resume until the 1919-20 season, by which time he had left Manchester United and moved on to Gillingham, back in the Southern League, where Bobby played the first twelve games of the season before losing his place. The following article appeared in the *Sheffield Independent* dated Thursday, 20 May 1920:

> *Robert Hughes Beale has resigned for Manchester United, and will be available when required next season. Beale left the United club just before the war to attend to his father's business at Maidstone. Last season he kept goal for Gillingham.*

Despite returning to Manchester United he made no more appearances for them. His father's business, referred to in the above article, was the family's undertaker business, W.T. Beale & Sons, in which he was one of the directors.

Randall Beale served during the First World War as a captain with the Royal Army Service Corps. He survived the war, dying in 10 May 1944 at the age of 64 at the West Kent General Hospital in Maidstone.

It does not appear that Alfred Beale served during the war. He emigrated to Sydney, Australia, leaving from London on board the TSS *Themistocles* on 6 June 1912. He married Nellie M. Ogden in Woollahra, New South Wales, in 1929, and passed away in Sydney on 26 November 1958. At the time of his death he was 76 years of age and living at 45 White Street, Balgowlah, New South Wales.

Lilian Bland was born in Maidstone on 22 September 1878 and went on to become both a journalist and an aviator. In her early twenties she began her journalistic career in London, working for many of the capital's newspaper titles as both a journalist and photographer. Her interest in aviation appears to have stemmed from around the mid-1880s when she received a postcard from her uncle William James Smythe who was holidaying in Paris, showing the Louis Bleriot monoplane. In early 1910 she built a glider from a combination of spruce, bamboo and cotton, which she named *Mayfly*. After a few alterations, a 20-horsepower engine was added and in late August 1910 at Randalstown, Co. Antrim, Bland managed to fly the *Mayfly* for what was described as 'a short hop off the ground'. With that few feet of flight, Bland became the first person and the first woman to fly an aircraft in Ireland, as well as making the *Mayfly* the first engine-powered bi-plane in Ireland.

Lilian Bland's Mayfly.

Despite her continuing progression and success with her flying enterprises, her father was extremely concerned for her safety and neither did he particularly believe that flying aircraft was something that a woman should be involved in. He managed to get her to give up aeronautics by buying her a car. But rather than just enjoying the experience of driving it, in April 1911 she opened and ran a car dealership in Belfast, which still wasn't something that her father saw as being suitable for a woman to be involved with. Six months later she married her cousin, Charles Loftus Bland, sold the car dealership, emigrated to Canada and helped her husband build up their newly acquired farm near Vancouver. She returned to England in 1935 and settled in Kent before later retiring to Cornwall, where she passed away on 11 May 1971 at 92 years of age. If there isn't a plaque commemorating her name on display somewhere in Maidstone, then maybe there should be.

Robert Peel Glanville Blatchford was born in Maidstone on 17 March 1851. His parents, John Glanville and Georgina Louisa Corri Blatchford, where both in the entertainment business, John as a 'strolling comedian' and Georgina as an actress. Robert was many things. To start with he was an atheist, which could, in some quarters of British society of the time, not have gone down too well. When Robert was only 2 years of age his father died leaving Georgina, Robert and Montagu to look after and provide for themselves, mainly through Georgina's acting, although Robert and Montagu helped by performing comedy routines with their mother. Robert senior was a military man, but long before the First World War. By the time he left the Army in 1878, he had worked

Robert Peel Glanville Blatchford.

his way up to the rank of sergeant major, having served with the 103rd Regiment of Foot which became the 2nd Battalion Royal Dublin Fusiliers, and the 96th Regiment of Foot which, under the Chilcot Reforms of 1881, became the 2nd Battalion, Manchester Regiment. By the time of the 1911 census, Robert was already 60 years of age, living at 321 Norwood Road, Herne Hill, London, and his occupation was shown as a publisher, journalist and author. He lived there with his wife Sarah and their three children Winnifred, Robert and Dorothea, and they had a housekeeper, Annie Cartwright.

Robert junior served during the First World War. He enlisted on 30 June 1915 when he became a private (10765) in the Queen's (Royal West Surrey) Regiment, before later transferring to the Army Service Corps, Mechanical Transport section, where he became private M/381490. He served in France, but didn't see out the end of the war as he was discharged from the Army for no longer being physically fit for war service, due to an unspecified, yet obviously debilitating, sickness. As was in keeping with the times, men who had served their country and had then been subsequently discharged due to wounds or sickness were provided by the War Office with an individually-numbered silver war badge which was to be worn on the lapel of a jacket. This would let other people know that the man wearing the badge had served his country and wasn't a 'shirker.' Robert's badge number was 411,271.

Robert senior was a socialist campaigner and held strong views and opinions on social issues of the day, on such matters as housing, education and job opportunities for those who needed them the most, usually the poorer and less well-off in society. With his journalistic head on, during the second week of December 1909 and five years before the outbreak of war, Robert wrote a series of articles for the *Daily Mail*, their theme being a warning of the threat of imperial Germany to the safety of Europe. One of the articles included the following:

> *I write these articles because I believe Germany is deliberately preparing to destroy the British Empire; and because I know that we are not ready or able to defend ourselves against a sudden and formidable attack. At the present moment the whole country is in ferment about the budget and the Peers and the Election. It seems sheer criminal lunacy to waste time and strength in chasing such political bubble when the existence of the Empire is threatened.*

The articles were read far and wide, and also came to the attention of those in government both in Britain and Germany. The Kaiser denounced Blatchford's protestations as being 'very mischievous and singularly ill timed'. The German press universally condemned the article. Blatchford even visited Germany before the war and on his return home wrote an article which included the following:

> *I am convinced that they will be plunged in to war without their will. I like Germany; I like German cities; and I like the German people. But I believe that the rulers of the German people are deliberately and cynically preparing them into a wicked and desperate war of conquest. The Germans cannot prevent the war, because they do not believe it is coming. The British could prevent that war if, before it is too late, they could be really convinced that it is coming. That is why I want to convince them that war is coming, because I want to prevent that horrible war.*

On the day Britain declared war on Germany, Blatchford wrote to his good friend and fellow founder of *The Clarion* newspaper, Alexander Mattock Thompson, who had been born in Karlsruhe in Germany to English parents but who had moved to Paris when he was only 5 years of age. His letter included the following:

> *I shall write a cautious article counselling peace and suggesting that the Secretary of State for Foreign Affairs, Sir Edward Grey, should ask Russia and Germany to suspend hostilities pending a friendly mediation by America, England and Italy, or any one of those powers. But I do not think really that European peace is possible until Germany has been defeated and humiliated. And I realise the great possibility that we shall be at war with Germany before the Clarion comes out. And I hope we are.*

Robert Blatchford was certainly a man of great foresight with an understanding of the political arena better than most politicians seem to have had at the time.

William Robert Brooks was born in Maidstone on 11 June 1844 and went on to become a world-renowned American astronomer who discovered at least twenty-six new comets in his lifetime, the first being in 1881 through a telescope he had made himself. His parents, William, who was a Baptist minister, and his mother Caroline, took the decision to emigrate to Marion, New York. As a young man growing up in his adopted country, he appeared to be interested in the vast array of technology that was being developed. In the nearby town of Phelps he became a photographer, which provided him with a deeper understanding of lens construction, which in turn led him in the direction of astronomy, for which he designed and built his own telescopes. Brooks is another fine example of the part Maidstone has played in shaping the world's technological advances.

Lady Victoria Buxton didn't have that much to do with Maidstone, but I feel that she is still worth a brief mention. Her parents were Charles Noel, the 1st Earl of Gainsborough and Lady Frances Jocelyn. During Victoria's younger years the family moved to Barham Court in the village of Teston, near Maidstone. The home was once that of Reginald Fitzurse, who was one of the knights who murdered Thomas Beckett in Canterbury Cathedral in 1170. Victoria grew up in the evangelical faith, a cornerstone of which was helping those who were less well off. With this at her core, she went on to become a philanthropist, recognized in particular for her work with the Young Women's Christian Association.

William Henry Cooper was born in Maidstone on 11 September 1849 and went on to become an international cricketer. The 1851 census shows him living at 7 Wyatt Street with his mother Elizabeth Cooper and her brother and sister, Henry and Mary Newman. He grew up in the town but moved to Australia as an adult. He didn't take up cricket until he was 27 years of age but within only four years he had been selected to play in a test match for Australia against England due in the main to his bowling prowess rather than his skill as a batsman. He only ever played in two test matches, the first in 1881 in Australian and the second three years later in England as part of the three-test series, which Australia lost.

Ernest Carpenter Elmore was born in Maidstone in 1901 and went on to become a theatre producer and director. He was probably better known as John Bude, under which name he wrote thirty crime novels with the main character in most of them being Inspector William Meredith. These were published over a period of twenty-three years between 1935 and 1958. He did write under his own name, in total he wrote a further seven novels between 1928 and 1954, with maybe his 1946 effort being the most oddly named – *Snuffy Snorty Dog*.

Frank Finn was born in Maidstone in 1868 and attended Maidstone Grammar School before continuing his studies at Oxford University. He went on to become a renowned ornithologist, writing numerous books on birds from all over the world.

Nigel Sydney Augustine Harrison was born in Maidstone on 29 November 1878 and went on to play first class cricket for London County in 1900. He also played for Durham in the Minor Counties Championship between 1902 and 1905. He was a military man but his service ended more than ten years before the outbreak of the First World War. In 1901 he served with the 1st Volunteer Brigade, part of the Durham Light Infantry, as a second lieutenant. He was promoted to the rank of lieutenant the following year and finally resigned his commission in February 1904.

Ethel Agnes Mary Moorhead was born in Maidstone on 28 August 1869. During the First World War she was heavily involved in the suffragette movement, mainly in Scotland where she had joined the Women's Social and Political Union. She also joined the Women's Freedom League, which encouraged women to find appropriate wartime work. She was very militant in her views and served several prison sentences, including one in Edinburgh in February 1914 when she became the first Scottish suffragette to be force fed.

Sir Hugh Garrard Tyrwhitt-Drake was an extremely interesting character. During the course of his lifetime, and in no particular order, he was an author, the High Sheriff of Kent, the Deputy Lieutenant of

Kent, a businessman, a zoo owner, Freeman of the Borough of Maidstone, and during the First World War he was the Mayor of Maidstone between 1915 and 1916 and on eleven other occasions. Remarkably, he spent a total of 48 years on the Borough of Maidstone Council. He was knighted in 1936 for his political and public services to both Maidstone and the County of Kent. He was a Maidstonian through and through, being born in the town on 22 May 1881 and dying there on 24 October 1964 when he was 83 years of age.

Sir Hugh lived in a lovely home called Cobtree Manor in Sanding which is a suburb to the north of Maidstone. It was in the grounds of this home that he maintained his zoo, keeping bears, elephants, lions and tigers. Up until 1934

Sir Hugh Garrard Tyrwhitt-Drake.

the zoo was an entirely private affair, but from then until its closure in 1959, it was open to the public. It was on the topic of animals that he wrote two books. The first in 1939, *Beasts and Circuses*: *My Life with Animals,* and the second, published seven years later in 1946, *The English Circus and Fairground*.

Hugh Granville White ended up as a Commander of the British Empire (CBE) and with the rank of Air Vice-Marshal. By the end of the First World War he was officially classified as a flying ace; he had been credited with seven aerial victories, or 'confirmed kills' as they were also referred to. He remained in the Royal Air Force after the war and went on to serve his country throughout the Second World War, finally retiring in 1955 at the age of 57. He was born in Maidstone on 1 March 1898 to parents Herbert and Beatrice White. He had an elder brother, Herbert Beresford White, and an elder sister, Margarita Beatrice White, both of whom had their own interesting wartime stories. Together they lived at 14 The Poplars, Tonbridge Road, Maidstone.

Hugh, at 17, became an officer cadet at the Royal Military College at Sandhurst. He acquired a commission with The Buffs (Royal East

Kent Regiment) on 7 April 1916, having just turning 18 and was almost immediately seconded to the Royal Flying Corps to undergo training to become a pilot at RFC Castle Bromwich in Birmingham where No.5 Reserve Squadron was based. He trained on both Maurice Farman Longhorn and Shorthorn aircraft and qualified as a pilot on 22 June 1916. Finally he had to undergo a further two weeks training at Norwich with the No.9 Reserve Squadron. Only then was he deemed sufficiently trained to be sent to No. 20 Squadron, Royal Flying Corps, where he quickly acquired the nickname of 'Child Pilot'. By the end of the war he had been credited with seven confirmed kills qualifying him as an ace. On the Flight Global website flightglobal.com, the following information is recorded in the first aero weekly journal entitled *Flight*. The edition is dated 15 February 1917. It includes a list of British officers who were wounded, killed, and those who were taken prisoner by the Germans. Under the list of those who had been reported as wounded in action was 2nd Lieutenant H.G. White, Buffs (E.Kent) att:d RFC. Although the extent of his wounds were not included in the article, they must have been minor as on 5 April 1917, back flying again, he recorded his first victory when, along with Private T. Allum who was acting as his observer in a FE2d two-seater aircraft, he forced down a German Albatros D.lll fighter. The pilot, Josef Flink, who had been wounded, was captured on landing. Some time after the beginning of June 1917, by which time he had claimed two more confirmed kills, he returned to England to serve as a flying instructor, initially with No.59 Training Squadron at RFC Yatesbury in Wiltshire, which was also used by No.7 and No.8 Squadrons of the Australian Flying Corps, and from November that year he moved on to No.38 Training Squadron at RFC Rendcomb, which is a quaint old village in the Cotswolds. He returned to France to once again undertake operational flying duties on 25 February 1918 when he joined No.29 Squadron RFC. Then on 22 May the same year, by which time the RFC and the RNAS had amalgamated to form the Royal Air Force, he once again returned to England to become a flying instructor, this time at No.9 Training Depot at RAF Shawbury near Shrewsbury. On 17 July he was appointed officer-in-charge of flying training at No.30 Training Depot at RAF Northolt in South Ruislip in West London. What made this so remarkable an achievement, was that he had just turned 20 years of age.

Herbert Beresford White was a lieutenant in the Royal Horse Artillery and Royal Field Artillery, which was part of the 23rd Brigade, when he was killed in action on 13 April 1917. He is buried at the Chocques Military Cemetery in the Pas-de-Calais. At the time of his death, he was 21 years of age.

Margarita Beatrice White's story wasn't really about her but who she married. Although the marriage didn't take place until after the war in 1921, the connection to her husband and the part he played in the war makes a worthwhile and relevant story. The man she married was Frederick Sowery.

Frederick Sowery had enlisted early on in the war on 31 August 1914 and was commissioned as a second lieutenant in the Royal Fusiliers, with whom he fought in France at the Battle of Loos where he was

Frederick Sowery.

wounded. He was returned to England where he spent three months in hospital having his wounds treated and convalescing. On his release in December 1915 he joined the Royal Flying Corps. As a pilot he went on to have a distinguished flying career receiving the DSO on 4 October 1917, the Military Cross on 23 November 1917, and the Air Force Cross on 1 January 1919.

The citation for his DSO appeared in a supplement to the *London Gazette* on 4 October 1916:

> *His Majesty the KING has been graciously pleased to appoint the undermentioned officers, Companions of the Distinguished Service Order, in recognition of their gallantry and distinguished service in connection with the successful attack on Enemy Airships.*

This related to the bringing down of the German Zeppelin *L-32* over Great Burstead near Billericay in Essex on 24 September 1915.

The citation for his MC appeared in a supplement to the *London Gazette* on 6 April 1918:

> *2nd Lt. (T/Capt) Frederick Sowery, DSO., R.Fus. and RFC. For conspicuous gallantry and devotion to duty in shooting down in less than two months two Albatross scouts and a Rumpler two seater and a Fokker scout, and in two engagements flying very low and engaging and scattering hostile infantry.*

His AFC was announced in a supplement to the *London Gazette* of 1 January 1919.

CHAPTER 8

The Voluntary Training Corps

Volunteer Training Corps were not a new invention and had been about for many years in different variations. But they all served the same purpose: protection of the realm.

During the war many towns formed their own Voluntary Training Corps, which were for men who, because of age, disability or commitments, were unable to enlist in either the regular Army or the Territorial Force, but who still wanted to do their bit. Nobody wanted to be thought of as a coward or a malingerer or to be one day asked by a grandchild, 'What did you do in the war, Grandad?'

As I mentioned in the earlier chapter on the first year of the war, Maidstone's Voluntary Training Corps came about largely because of the meeting about recruitment that was held at Maidstone Town Hall on 9 December 1914 chaired by Mr A.P. Hedges. It struck him in connection with the Volunteer Training Corps movement that they had a number of men who, because of their age or infirmity, were unable to enlist in His Majesty's Armed forces. Despite their inabilities, these men still wanted to do their bit for their country in its time of need. Many of them were veterans, who had previously served their country in places such as South Africa or India.

Mr Hedges spoke of preparation rather than a wait-and-see approach. He didn't want people to become complacent and rely on a belief that the Germans would not invade Great Britain. He drew the analogy of a wounded animal who had no other option but to come out fighting for its very survival, which in turn made it an extremely dangerous and unpredictable beast. He didn't see the war being won or lost in the short term, but over a longer period of time, and that more and more men would gradually be needed on the home front to replace the younger and more able-bodied men who would be needed to go off and fight. These would be the very men who made up the Voluntary Training Corps.

Mr Hedges said to those present at Maidstone Town Hall that he fully appreciated it was easy for someone like him to make a speech on the topic and word it in such a way that it would sound patriotic and compelling, but he wasn't trying to cajole or embarrass anyone. He was simply giving them the facts, that it was then down to each man to decide for himself what he should or shouldn't do, and that, when the war was over, no man should be found wanting when asked by a friend, colleague or relative, what part they played in the war. At the end of the meeting it was unanimously decided to form a Volunteer Training Corps for the Maidstone and District area.

By Friday, 18 December 1914, the newly-formed Maidstone & District Volunteer Training Corps had already been put through its first course of training. Amongst those present on this auspicious occasion were the Deputy Mayor of Maidstone, Councillor A.T. Epps, who had previously served with the West Kent Yeomanry, Councillor S. Dyke, and a number of local prominent professional gentlemen.

On 23 December Lord Harris, Vice-Lieutenant of Kent, issued on behalf of the Lord Lieutenant of Kent, the Marquis Camden, who at the time was away serving with his regiment, instructions as to what the civil population of Kent should do in the event of an invasion by German forces. The instructions were initially announced at the Sessions House in Maidstone. This directly connected to the Volunteer

Training Corps, which caused Lord Harris to remind people of a recent government announcement on the matter concerning the inherent dangers for individual civilians drawn to act on their own in the event of such an invasion. In order to be recognized as a combatant an individual needed to be a member of a Volunteer Corps which had been affiliated to the Central Association of Volunteer Training Corps which was situated at the Royal Courts of Justice in London. Each member of such Corps was issued by the government with a badge which effectively identified them as a combatant to an enemy. Civilians who were not in possession of the government badge could not be classed as a 'combatant' and would be expected to carry out non-combatant duties. Such individuals would also have to surrender any firearms which they had in their possession, as failure to do so could result in them being shot by invading German forces if they were captured.

On Monday, 22 February 1915, a conference took place at Maidstone which had been convened by Lord Harris, the Vice-Lieutenant of Kent, in relation to the Volunteer Training Corps movement across the county. This was certainly not a meeting to be missed. Lord Northbourne and the majority of the county's Deputy Lieutenants were all in attendance. Lord Harris included the following in his address to the conference:

> *I understand that what is sought by the Corps formed in Kent, is that a scheme of centralization should be introduced, that is to say, that there should be a linking up of existing Corps into Battalions and of Battalions into Regiments. If that is done you will quite understand that there must be a centralized control, and I am prepared to propose a scheme very similar in character to those that have been adopted in other counties.*

Lord Harris was proposing that Volunteer Training Corps units all over the county had to be able to work in unison with each other. If they had different rank and unit structures and strengths as well as different operating procedures, this would not be possible. He suggested to the conference that a Volunteer Training Corps central committee should be set up, principally composed of the Deputy Lieutenants of Kent. Whether the individuals concerned had any military experience, and if they did, did they also possess any knowledge of up-to-date military tactics, is unclear. Lord Harris continued:

> *Each Deputy Lieutenant should take one or more of the Corps already formed and be its guide, philosopher, friend and the connecting link between the local Corps and Headquarters. I propose to adopt for these officials the old title connected with the Army, 'Commissary.' Their duties would have nothing to do as Commissaries, with your military efficiency further than the encouragement they might be able to give you. Their duties would rather be to assist you and to some extent control you as regards finance, as regards the men you enlist, and as regards the rules that you would have to observe. The responsibility for your military efficiency would rest with the Inspecting Officers whom the Central Association would appoint, and it is quite possible that some member of the Central Committee might be both Commissary and an Inspecting Officer.*

It could be argued that Lord Harris's suggestions in relation to deputy lieutenants and making them commissaries was no more than a case of jobs for the boys – a position that would validate what they did during the war and one which would place them in a relatively important position while not having to take any responsibility for the overall efficiency of their particular Corps. The commissary for Harrietsham & Maidstone, was Colonel J C Campbell. Lord Harris provided more detail concerning his proposal:

> *Now my scheme as regards distribution is to make use of the ancient divisions of the county, East, Mid, West, and to have a Regiment for each, the three Regiments forming the Kent Brigade. The Brigade must have a title, and I have again fallen back upon ancient nomenclature and suggest 'The Kent Brigade of Volunteer Fencibles'.*

By March 1915 the County of Kent already had some forty-eight Volunteer Training Corps units and by October the same year there were an estimated 10,000 members across the county. They wore a khaki uniform and were distinguishable from any branch of the military by the wearing of a red armlet with the black letters 'GR', which stood for Georgius Rex, King George V. Some who questioned the Volunteers' usefulness, preferred to call them 'Grandpa's Regiment' or 'Genuine Relics'. An armlet was individual to the man wearing it, with both a number and his name recorded on it.

Each regiment consisted of a number of battalions drawn from across the county, and most towns had their own Corps which consisted of up to thirty men, with two or more sections forming a company, all of whom had to follow the regulations as set out by the Central Association.

Section: There were usually 4 sections, with 15 men in each, which made up a platoon.
Platoon: There were usually 4 platoons, with 60 men in each, which made up a company.
Company: There were between 4 and 6 companies of 240 to 300 men, which made up a Battalion.
Battalion: A number of battalions made up a regiment.

Being a member of a Volunteer Training Corps was a real commitment, not just because of what each man had to do, but also because they usually had to provide their own uniforms, at their own expense.

On Wednesday, 21 April 1915, Colonel Warde, the Member of Parliament for Mid-Kent, inspected the Maidstone and District Volunteer Training Corps in connection with the Kent Fencibles scheme which had been inaugurated by Lord Harris. He was suitably impressed with what he witnessed.

With the Military Service Act of 1916 came conscription which empowered the Military Service Tribunals to direct men to join the Volunteer Training Corps. However, because the Volunteer Act of 1863 had never been repealed, men who had been made to join the Corps could then use a clause from the 1863 Act that allowed them to resign within fourteen days. The Volunteer Act 1916 was swiftly brought in to close this loophole, preventing members from resigning from the Corps for the duration of the war.

Of the 285,000 Volunteers in February 1918, more than 100,000 of them were there because they had been ordered to enrol by a Military Service Tribunal.

The *Essex & Sussex Courier* of 10 March 1916 reported that the Volunteer Training Corps had finally received the full recognition of the government on a national level, for which they had been waiting. It was hoped that this would encourage those qualified men who had previously refrained from joining the volunteers to at last take that leap of faith and enrol in large numbers. One of the reasons that the government had been tepid in its approval and support for the Corps was the belief that able-bodied men who were suitable to undertake military service would try to prevent their conscription into the military by joining the VTC instead.

In October 1916 the Volunteers were issued with new badges of rank, cap badges and shoulder adornments. These replaced the VTC insignia. The change meant that all ranks, officers and men alike, wore the same cap badge, in the shape of the Royal coat of arms, with officers wearing the letter V in place of collar badges. Other ranks wore the name of their county, along with the letter V.

The topic of Volunteer Training Corps was discussed in the House of Commons on Tuesday 7 November 1917. It was reported in *The Scotsman* the following day that the Financial Secretary to the War Office stated that the Volunteer Training Corps were intended for home and local defence. The question of government assistance was under consideration and he hoped that he would soon be in a position to make a statement on the subject.

Having finally realised the benefits of the Corps to the country, the government finally acted and made the War Office responsible for them, providing them with uniforms, P14 Enfield Rifles, and machine guns. Their rank structure became the same as that of the Army, the original Central Association was disbanded, and they were placed under the control of the Territorial Association.

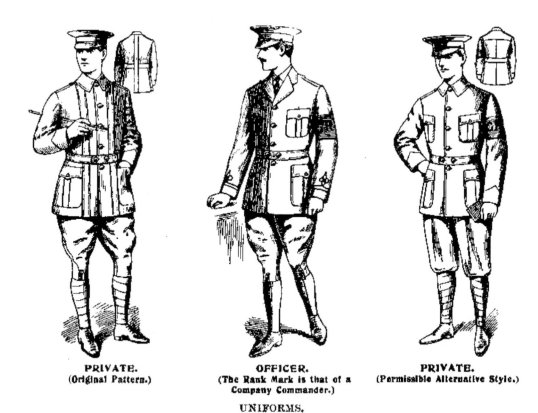

PRIVATE.
(Original Pattern.)

OFFICER.
(The Rank Mark is that of a
Company Commander.)

PRIVATE.
(Permissible Alternative Style.)

UNIFORMS.

Volunteer Training Corps uniforms.

Lord Harris, in his capacity as the commandant of the Kent Volunteer Regiment, sent a letter to the mayors of Kent County Boroughs and the chairmen of Urban and Rural Councils, dated Friday 23 February 1917. The letter was sent from the regiment's headquarters in Union Street, Maidstone. It said how important the regiment was and spoke of the need to qualify men to serve in it as more and more men were being sent off to fight in the war and because Military Service Tribunals were refusing more and more exemptions.

Lord Harris asked employers to allow their workers freely to enrol in the Volunteer Corps. He pointed out that because of the county's geographical location, if there were an invasion Kent would be at the front of the action, and in such circumstances men wouldn't be expected to be at their place of work but doing their bit in defence of the realm. So, he said, it was imperative that all were allowed the necessary time for training.

In the early part of October 1917, the Marquis Camden, the Lord Lieutenant of Kent, and Lord Harris, announced a scheme to form a Medical Volunteer Corps, which would be incorporated into the already established Volunteer Training Corps. If a German invasion did take place, and men of the Volunteer Training Corps fought bravely and valiantly against them, then there would undoubtedly be large numbers of casualties that would need tending to, so it made perfect sense to have a section that were medically trained to undertake such a role.

Members of the Maidstone Volunteer Training Corps, in keeping with other sections around the country, were used for a range of different tasks. They guarded vulnerable locations, dug anti-invasion defences, helped with the transport of wounded prisoners, and at times even assisted with harvesting crops.

By 1918 the threat of a German invasion of the United Kingdom had long since subsided, but the men of the Maidstone Volunteer Corps had quietly done their bit to ensure the safety of the people in their community. In the end they thankfully were not required to fight the German Army, but if they had have been, they no doubt would have done a sterling job.

The Volunteer Training Corps was finally disbanded in October 1920, the need for it well and truly over, at least for the next nineteen years. The Corps' motorized battalions were kept until 1921, mainly to be used in cases of civil unrest. Members of the Corps were not awarded service medals for wartime participation. For their efforts, they received a certificate.

CHAPTER 9

Hayle Place, Maidstone VAD

Voluntary Aid Detachments across the country played an extremely important part during the First World War. They provided much needed respite for weary soldiers who were recovering from their wounds. They preferred the more relaxed atmosphere of the VAD hospitals, where they weren't under the strict discipline of Army regulations.

Most towns and cities, especially those along the south coast of England, had at least one VAD hospital, as everybody pulled together wanting to do their bit for the war effort on the home front. Volunteers carried out a multitude of tasks, from working on the wards, to being cooks, cleaners, orderlies or working in canteens. They might also be mechanics or ambulance drivers, roles that were more likely to be done by men. Some worked full time while others were part time. Some were paid while others worked without any pay at all.

The Red Cross website has a search facility which makes it possible to look for an individual's service record, where they lived, where they worked, the time they worked for the VAD, and which duties they carried out.

For the people of Maidstone, working for the VAD so that their skills could best serve their community was a big issue, it was almost a point of honour. There are over 700 names on the list, people who were either from Maidstone or who worked in VAD hospitals in

Hayle Place.

Maidstone. Here are just three examples of the individuals who supported the VAD organisation, where they lived and what it was that they did, so that you the reader can have a flavour of what information is available, and you can do your own research if you wish:

Miss Millicent Atkins Burnaby worked at Hayle Place in Maidstone, or, to give it its official title, Kent 14. She had previously worked at Quarry Hill hospital, Kent 148. Her time in Maidstone was spent working as a cook. In total she worked 4,763 hours for the VAD between November 1914 and March 1919. She wasn't from Maidstone, her home was in Tonbridge, but as was common with personnel who worked for the VAD during the war, many didn't work in the town where they lived.

Mrs Violet Emily Allfrey worked for VAD Kent 14. She lived at Bensfords in Boughton Monchelsea and worked at Hayle Place Hospital in Maidstone part time as a pantry maid for just a month in November and December 1917. She had two sons, Richard and Hubert, and her husband Charles Moubray Allfrey was a major in the 3rd Battalion, Royal West Kent Regiment. He first arrived in France in November 1915 and served for the rest of the war, finally returning to his family after the fighting was over. They were an affluent family, having a chauffeur, groom, nursery maid and three other servants.

William Anslow lived at 55 Salisbury Avenue, Maidstone, and served with Kent VAD 55. He began working at No. 12 VAD Hospital in August 1915 and remained there until after the war was over. His duties included working nights, air raid duties and helping out with convoys of wounded prisoners arriving at the nearby railway station.

The work that was carried out by these people was truly amazing and inspiring. For most, they did it without any pay, even though most had a full-time job and a household to look after, and they had to conform to a strict code of discipline while working for the VAD.

CHAPTER 10

Those Who Served and Returned

This will not be a complete list, and neither is it intended to be. It is just a brief look at a few individuals whom I have selected at random. The British Army's pension records for the First World War show that a total of 1,136 men who had connections with Maidstone returned home, either during the war or after it was over. I believe that those who survived and returned home deserve a mention just as much as those who died.

Here are just a few of those Maidstone men who made it back home, to a world of hope and belief of a better tomorrow, coupled with a trace of doubt of just exactly what it was that lay ahead, while mourning the loss of their friends and comrades who weren't so fortunate. Some of these men were still serving at the end of the war while others had been discharged during the war for no longer being fit enough for war service, which usually meant that they had been wounded, or suffered from an illness which prevented them from serving as a soldier.

If I have not mentioned somebody who you know, then I apologise. Nothing should be inferred from any such omission. There are a few war memorials around the country that include the names of every man from the community or parish who served, regardless of whether they returned or not. As I have said, these are just a few individuals whom

I have selected at random to help provide an overall picture of those who returned home.

It is usually the men who served in their country's military forces during the war, survived and returned home to their loved ones who history forgets. It is those who died as a result of their involvement in the war who history records and commemorates.

Roy Backhurst Abbott lived at 63 King Edward Road in Maidstone with his parents, John and Mary, and his elder sister Gladys. There were three older children, Violet, Jack and May, but they had all left home by the time Roy was 16. After leaving school, he became a clerk in a local tailoring business. His brother Jack had also gone into the tailoring business, where he became a draper's assistant in Leeds, Yorkshire, but I could not find a definitive record of him having served during the war. I did however find in the British Army Rolls medals for the First World war a card which showed the name J.S. (Stannard being Jack's middle name) Abbott, who served as a private (IG/15761) in the Buffs (East Kent Regiment). Roy became a private (265373) in the Kent Cycle Battalion of the Buffs East Kent Regiment. He was nearly 22 years of age when he enlisted at Tonbridge on 25 June 1916. Although originally he was allocated to the 2nd/5th Battalion, Home Counties Field Ambulance, as a private (2418), this was changed before he'd even completed his basic training, and he ended up serving with the 3rd Battalion, The Buffs (East Kent Regiment). Roy went to France as part of the British Expeditionary Force with the regiment's 3rd and 6th Battalions between 16 December 1916 and 17 May 1917. He then returned to the United Kingdom where he was posted to the 'Depot', but in less than two weeks he had been once again posted to the 3rd Battalion where he remained until he was demobilized on 2 October 1919. Roy lived until the age of 73, passing away in March 1968 in Sudbury, Suffolk.

Harold Graham Allard had enlisted in the Army on 8 February 1909 at Camberwell, Surrey, just after his 18th birthday, when he signed up as a private (434) with the 21st County of London Battalion of the London Regiment which was a Territorial unit. At five feet eleven inches in height he was noticeably tall for his age. At the time he was serving an apprenticeship as a draper's assistant with Jones & Higgins Tailors of 9 Hanover Park, Peckham, South East London. Part of the commitment to the Territorial Force was to undertake an annual training camp. In 1911 this was undertaken at the Shorncliffe Army camp near Folkestone and the following year at Aldershot. Sadly, Harold failed to attend either camp and his military record was marked up accordingly as being 'Absent' on both occasions. Annoyed and disappointed by what was seen to be his lack of commitment, a decision was taken that he should be discharged, and on New Year's Eve 1912 his record was marked, 'Discharged in consequence of – Absentee – Struck Off'. He had served for 3 years and 325 days but, sadly for him, it counted for nothing. Whether or not Harold subsequently re-enlisted in the regular Army at the outbreak of the war is something that I have not been able to establish, but if he did, then he survived. Records show that on 29 June 1936, at the age of 45, he took up a position with the Great Western Railway Company.

Thomas Andrews was born in Maidstone in 1873. He enlisted in the Army with the 3rd Battalion, The Buffs (East Kent Regiment) on 5 September 1914, at Maidstone. He became Private 212 and was placed on the Army Reserve (Special Reservists). He was discharged on 20 December 1916 after having served for 2 years and 111 days for no longer being physically fit enough for war service under King's Regulations.

Stephen Bance was 22 years of age when he enlisted at Maidstone on 6 February 1915 and became a private (G/10673) in the 3rd Battalion Royal West Kent Regiment. He was discharged just five months later on 4 July 1915 for no longer being physically fit enough for wartime service. His Army service record did not elaborate on the ailment he had which resulted in him having to be discharged, other than at his initial medical it was noted that he had a minor problem with his left knee, but it was deemed not to be sufficient to cause him to fail his medical. He was only 18 years of age. Five months later his military career was over, a decision which possibly saved his life.

Frederick Ashby has an interesting story. He enlisted on 10 November 1914 at Bromley, which straight away appears somewhat strange. Why enlist at Bromley when there was a recruitment office in

Maidstone where Frederick lived? He became a private (4375) in the Royal West Kent Regiment, but just eight days later he transferred to the Royal West Surrey Regiment as Private G/3681. He originally served with the 3rd Battalion, transferred to the 1st Battalion on 2 February 1915, and ended up in the 10th Battalion, from which he was discharged on 5 March 1916. He hadn't been wounded, he wasn't suffering from any illness or disease, and his levels of fitness weren't sufficient to warrant his discharge on medical grounds. He was discharged under Paragraph 392 (V1) of the King's Regulations for making a mis-statement as to his age on enlistment, which he claimed was 19 years and 9 months. He was actually serving in France when his true age was discovered and was sent back to England on 3 March 1916. It wasn't made clear exactly how old Frederick was, but he could have been as young as 15 when he enlisted.

William George Adams was 21 years of age when he enlisted on 14 November 1914 at Maidstone and became a driver (T4/238843) in the Kent Brigade Company, Army Service Corps, which was a Territorial unit. His home address was shown as being 8 Fisher Street, Maidstone. He was discharged from the Army on 26 July 1916 so that he could enlist in the Royal Flying Corps. I could find no record of him having been killed during the war so I presume that he survived.

Powell Ambrose 'joined' on 8 July 1916 at Maidstone when he was 38 years of age. Besides being a gardener he was also on the Army Reserve list before he joined up as a private (3339) in the 3/1st Battalion, Royal East Kent Mounted Rifles, but on 11 November 1916, he transferred to the 2/1st Battalion, Royal East Kent Yeomanry, and six months after that he was discharged from the Army for no longer being physically fit enough for war service. He was a married man who lived at School Cottages, Lenham, with his wife Lily and their six children.

This is just a very few of the men who were either born or lived in Maidstone or whose parents lived there before or during the war, and who served in the armed forces and who either returned home after the war, or who for one reason or another were discharged before the fighting was over.

These were the men who survived, the ones who made it back home to be with their loved ones, some never again to talk about their experiences and memories of that war, the horror and carnage that they had witnessed and been involved in. Some of them had seen at first-hand how inhumane other human beings could be, they had witnessed a side of humanity which they had never wanted to see, and never wanted to see again. Once home, all they wanted to do was to forget and carry on with their lives the best that they could, in the hope that there would be a better tomorrow.

CHAPTER 11

Those Who Died

Maidstone Grammar School has a proud history stretching back nearly seven hundred years. To celebrate the memories of its former pupils who fell during the First World War, it has two wooden Rolls of Honour situated in its main hall. They record the names of the forty-three old Maidstonians who paid the ultimate price for their bravery.

Charles Ivo Barker was a second lieutenant in the 6th Battalion Queen's Own (Royal West Kent Regiment). He was 24 years of age when he was wounded in action on 14 March 1916, before passing away three days later. He is buried at the Bethune Town Cemetery which is located in the Pas-de-Calais. Before the war he had been but a humble cabinet salesman. It has always struck me how ordinary peace-loving young men had to change their lives so drastically when the fighting began, to kill and watch their friends being killed. His parents, Levi and Harriet Barker, lived at Shergold Cottage, Loose, Maidstone.

C.I. Barker.

J.L. Barling is almost certainly a mistake and should in fact be James Hollely Barling who was a pupil at Maidstone Grammar School between September 1894 and April 1900, leaving when he was 18 years of age. He was also born in Maidstone and it was where he lived for most of his life. In 1901 the family are shown as living at 7 High

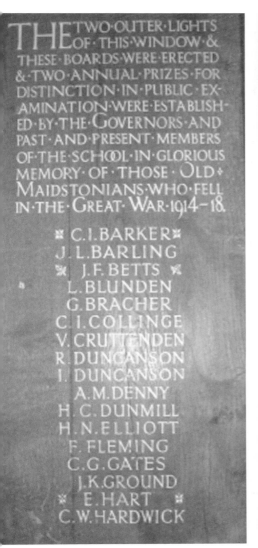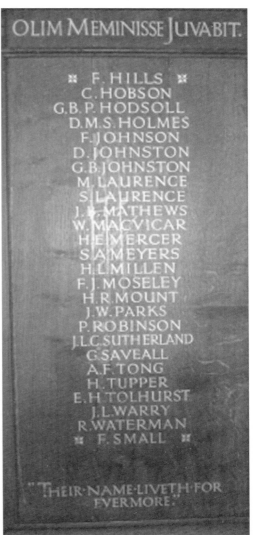

Maidstone Grammar School Roll of Honour.

Street, Maidstone, but ten years later in 1911 the family had moved to 78 Bank Street in the town, and it would appear that James's father, also called James, had by now passed away. The 1911 census shows

James as being a retired Watch and Clock Maker and Gold and Silversmith. James was a private (202238) in the 1st/4th Battalion, The Buffs, East Kent Regiment. The battalion was sent out to India in November 1914 where it remained for the duration of the war with the exception of a six-month tour in Aden between August 1915 and February 1916. By 1919 a number of men from the battalion were still serving in India and saw active service in the Third Afghan war. James died in Bengal on 16 June 1919 while serving with his Battalion in India. He is buried at the Ferozepore Military Cemetery.

John Percy Betts, Jack to his friends, served as a corporal (270991) with 'C' Company, 10th (Royal East Kent and West Kent Yeomanry) Battalion, The Buffs (East Kent Regiment). He was killed in action on 6 August 1918 aged 26 and is buried at the Saint-Venant Robecq Road British Cemetery, which is situated in the Pas-de-Calais. His bravery in the field had seen him awarded the Military Medal. Prior to the war he lived with his parents, James and Florence Betts, at Greenhill Farm, Otham, Maidstone, where James carried on his business as a farmer and butcher. He had four brothers and two sisters. His elder brother, Archibald, died in 1910 at the age of 21. Kenneth, who was born in 1903, was too young to have served in the war. I could find no trace of Herbert having served, who by the end of the war would have been 20.

His other brother, Laurence Betts, did serve in the war, arriving at Gallipoli on 24 September 1915 as a lance corporal (1440) with the West Kent Yeomanry which in March 1917 amalgamated with the East Kent Yeomanry to become the 10th (Yeomanry) Battalion, The Buffs (East Kent Regiment). This saw Laurence promoted to the rank of sergeant (270760). On 17 June 1918 he received a commission with the RAF, where he held the rank of second lieutenant. He survived the war and passed away in March 1982 aged 91.

Lewis Blunden attended Maidstone Grammar School between 1908 and 1915 and was a popular student, captaining both the school's football and cricket elevens. He also played in the school's

L. Blunden.

band. The family home was in Stockings Lane, Mill Street, Maidstone. He was a second lieutenant in the 5th (Cinque Ports) Battalion, Royal Sussex Regiment, which was a Territorial unit, when he was killed in action on 22 July 1916 aged 30. He is buried in the Bouzincourt Communal Cemetery Extension, which is situated in the Somme region of France.

Guy Bracher was a second lieutenant in the 6th Battalion, The Buffs (East Kent Regiment). He was 26 years of age when he died on 3 July 1916, the third day of the Battle of the Somme. He is buried at the Aveluy Communal Cemetery Extension in the Somme.

Herbert Stonehouse Coles was a captain in the 1st Battalion, Royal Welsh Fusiliers, when he was killed in action on 16 May 1915. He has no known grave and his name is commemorated on the Le Touret Memorial in the Pas-de-Calais. He was also a popular pupil during his years spent at Maidstone Grammar School, representing them at both football and cricket. His name was added to the school's Roll of Honour as recently as 2014.

H.S. Coles.

Charles Ingham Collinge had attended Maidstone Grammar School between 1910 and 1915, at which time he served as part of the Maidstone Officer Training Corps. He lived with his parents, John and Henrietta Collinge, at the School House, Larkfield, Kent. He enlisted on 28 February 1916 at Bisley, initially as a gunner (2798) in the Machine Gun Corps. His service record shows that he was admitted to the Auxiliary Military Hospital in Frodsham, Cheshire, on 21 November 1916, but it doesn't show why, or for how long. Reading further through his service record there is a slightly contradictory report, stating that he was wounded in the thigh on 29 October 1916 and admitted to a Field Hospital. On 2 November he was then treated by the 134 Field Ambulance, and on 5 November 1916 he was treated at number 9 Casualty Clearing Station before returning to England by ambulance train and the hospital ship *Asturias* on 18 November.

He was a flight lieutenant in 216 Squadron, Royal Flying

HM-S Asturias.

Corps/Royal Air Force. The Commonwealth War Graves Commission website records that he had previously served with the Tank Corps. His Army service record shows that at the time he received his temporary commission for duties with the Royal Flying Corps he was serving as a private (201281) with 'G' Battalion, the Tank Corps. It was while serving with them that he was wounded in 1917, having arrived in France on 25 May that year. He transferred to the Royal Flying Corps (317319) on 26 January 1918. He was then automatically transferred into the Royal Air Force under the provisions of the Air Force Constitution Act 1917 on 1 April 1918, initially as a flight cadet, before receiving his commission on 27 October 1918. This was reported in the *London Gazette* on 12 November 1918. He was flying a Handley Page F304 heavy bomber aircraft to Egypt on 25 July 1919 when he crashed in the sea off Monterosso in Italy, and drowned. He is buried in the Ravenna War Cemetery.

Vallance Cruttenden attended Maidstone Grammar School between 1900 and 1903. His father Edgar was the publican of the Brenchley Arms in Upper Stone Street. The 1911 census shows Vallance already serving in the Royal Navy as a 24-year-old 2nd writer, stationed at

HMS *Ganges*, a Majesty's Royal Naval Training establishment at Shotley near Ipswich. He went on to become a chief writer (347357) on HMS *Raglan* and had previously been mentioned in despatches for his actions. On 20 January 1918 the *Raglan* and other vessels of the Allied Aegean Squadron were attacked by the Turkish Battlecruiser *Yavuz Sultan Selim,* the light cruiser *Midilli*, along with other Turkish vessels in what became known as the Battle of Imbros. During the attack the *Raglan* was sunk with the loss of 127 of her crew, Vallance Cruttenden being one of them. Despite knowing the perilous

V. Cruttenden.

situation the ship was in, Cruttenden 'remained at his post, so as to decode a wireless signal for Commander Viscount Broome'. He was a married man who left behind a wife and 4-year-old son. Despite their sad loss they must have been proud of what Vallance did on that day. His body was one of those recovered and he was buried at the Lancashire Landing Cemetery in Turkey.

Roy Duncanson was 25 years of age and a second lieutenant in the 3rd Battalion, Duke of Wellington's (West Riding) Regiment, when he was killed in action a week in to the Battle of the Somme on 7 July 1916. His body was never recovered and his name is commemorated on the Thiepval Memorial.

Ian Ferguson Duncanson was 21 years of age and a second lieutenant in the 8th (The Argyllshire) Battalion, Princess Louise's Argyll and Sutherland Highlanders, which was a Territorial unit, when he was killed in action on 12 October 1917, leading his men 'over the top'. He is buried at the Poelcapelle British Cemetery, West-Vlaanderen, Belgium.

Ian's brother Roy Duncanson, also an ex-Maidstonian, was also a second lieutenant. He served with 3rd Battalion, Duke of Wellington's (West Riding) Regiment, but was attached to the 9th Battalion when he was killed in action on 7 July 1916. He has no known grave and is commemorated on the Thiepval Memorial.

Roy's and Ian's sister, Una Marguerite Duncanson, who was a nurse working with a Voluntary Aid Detachment serving in Egypt, died on 31 December when the hospital ship that she was serving on was torpedoed by a German submarine.

Their parents, James and Anne Duncanson, lived at Pimps Court, Tovil, in Maidstone after the war, but in the 1911 census the family had been living at Langley Park Farm, Langley, in Maidstone. They had six other children, three sons and three other daughters.

Arthur Martin Denny was a pupil at Maidstone Grammar School between 1896 and 1903. When war came he enlisted and became a rifleman (5600) with the 9th Battalion, London Regiment (Queen Victoria's Rifles). He was sent back from France to have his wounds treated at the Red Cross hospital in Salisbury, Wiltshire where he died of his wounds on 29 October 1916. He is buried at the Hanwell City of Westminster Cemetery in London. The 1901 census shows a 13-year-old Arthur living with his parents, John and Louisa Denny, and his elder sister Olive. The family were affluent enough to be able to employ a domestic servant. Arthur married Rose Dean on 11 March 1916 at the Parish Church of Saint Stephen, close to where they lived at 17 Drayton Grove, West Ealing. Sadly, because of the war they would never even celebrate their first anniversary.

A.M. Denny.

H.C. Dunmill is, I believe, Courtenay Dunmill. He was a corporal (14915) in the 212th Battery, Royal Field Artillery, which was part of the 2nd Brigade. They arrived in France in September 1914 and remained on the Western Front for the rest of the war. Courtenay died on 18 May 1918. As he is buried at Maidstone Cemetery it can be guessed that he was wounded abroad and sent back to England for further treatment.

Harry Nathaniel Elliott was a pupil at Maidstone Grammar School between 1899 and 1905. When war broke out, Harry was a clerk working for his father's flour mill company. He enlisted and initially served with the Royal Army Ordnance Corps as a private (013939) before later transferring to the Lancaster Fusiliers, also serving as a private (47093), with the regiment's 10th Battalion. He was 30 years of age when he was killed in action on 21 March 1918 during fighting in Flanders. Harry has no known grave and his name is commemorated on the Arras Memorial in the Pas-de-Calais. His parents, Edward and Mary Elliot, lived at 6 Albion Place in Maidstone with their elder son William and their three daughters, Marion, Dorothy and Florence. The family also employed a servant girl, Minnie Isac, who was 18. There were some interesting variations with this entry. Maidstone Grammar School have the surname spelled Elliot. The First World War medal rolls index cards also have the spelling as Elliot and show his service number as 47093. The Commonwealth War Graves Commission website have the spelling as Elliott and show his service number as 40649. The 1911 census clearly shows the surname spelt as Elliott, but all of the above references are for the same man. It just goes to show the difficulties that can arise by just one letter being omitted or added to a person's name.

Frank Fleming was a pupil at Maidstone Grammar School for just the one year in 1907 when he was 13 years of age. During the First World War he was commissioned as a second lieutenant in the beautifully-named 4th (Ross Highland) Battalion (Territorial), Seaforth Highlanders (Ross-shire Buffs, the Duke of Albany's), which came into existence in 1881 as a result of the Childers Reforms.

Frank's battalion first landed in France at Le Havre in November 1914 as part of the 152nd Brigade in the 51st Highland Division. He was killed in action while fighting on the Western Front in Belgium on 11 April 1918. He is one of the many young men who have no known graves, and is remembered by the inscription of his name on the Tyne Cot Memorial.

Charles Gillespie Gates was a pupil at Maidstone Grammar School for three years between 1904 and 1907. He enlisted in the Army during the war and became a corporal (19291) in the 6th Battalion, Queen's Own (Royal West Kent Regiment). He was 25 years of age when he was killed in action during fighting near Arras on 9 April 1917. He is buried at the Feuchy Chapel British Cemetery, at Wancourt in the

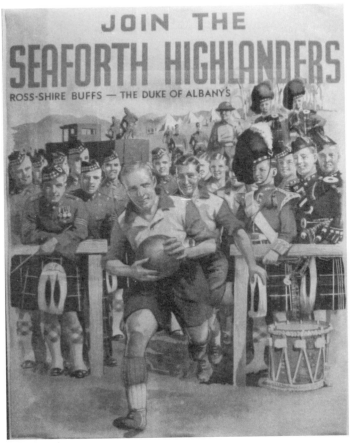

Seaforth Highlanders recruiting poster.

Pas-de-Calais. Before the war Charles, who was the youngest of five sons born to Frederick and Emma Gates, was working as a clerk for a wholesale grocer in Maidstone. The family lived at 77 Holland Road. Charles was attested and swore his oath of allegiance on 5 December 1915 at Maidstone, initially being allocated to the 4th Battalion, Queen's Own (Royal West Kent Regiment) and his service number was 3926. He was promoted to the rank of lance corporal on 22 June 1916, arrived in France on 13 January 1917, and a month later on 12 February was further promoted to the rank of corporal. Thirteen days before his death, he was disciplined and reprimanded for neglect of duty, for failing to relieve his sentries at the proper time while on active service. Of his four brothers, Frederick, Harry, Horace and Ernest, only Horace served during the war. On 15 October 1919 the eldest of Charles's brothers, Frederick, wrote a letter to the records officer of the Queen's Own (Royal West Kent Regiment) in Maidstone informing them that none of the family now lived at 77 Holland Road and that their parents had both passed away in January 1918.

Ivan John Kingston Ground was 29 years of age and a second lieutenant in the 10th Battalion, Queen's Own (Royal West Kent Regiment), when he was killed in action on 19 June 1916. The National Probate Calendar of Wills and Administration records that he died in France but he is buried just over the border at Tancrez Farm Cemetery in Belgium. He left behind a widow, Eleanor. John came from a relatively affluent family. Before the war he lived at 1 Ashford Road, Maidstone, with his parents, Edward, who was a 'doctor of medicine', his mother Eleann, his elder brother Ernest, who was an art student, his younger sister Fanny, as well as two servants who looked after the family. Maidstone Grammar School records show the name Ivan John Kingston Ground, but the 1911 census has the name written as just John Kingston Ground as does the Commonwealth War Graves website.

There are forty-nine men with the name Ernest Hart listed on the Commonwealth War Graves Commission website. The one I am looking for was a pupil at the Maidstone Grammar School between 1905 and 1909.

During the First World War, he served his King and country as a sergeant (12262) in the 7th Battalion, Norfolk Regiment, and when he was killed in action on 13 October 1915 he was only 24 years of age. His parents, Stephen and Mary Hart, lived at 55 Milton Street, Maidstone, with his brother Albert.

C.W. Hardwick is, I believe, Oswald *Ernest Hart.*

William Hardwick who attended Maidstone Grammar School for two years between 1907 and 1909. He enlisted in the earlier part of the war and was commissioned as a second lieutenant in the 1st Battalion, Devonshire Regiment. He was 25 years of age when he was killed in action on 9 May 1917 while serving on the Western Front, has no known grave, and is commemorated on the Arras Memorial. Oswald's father, Frederick Septimus Hardwick, a physician and a surgeon, and mother Emma, had another son who according to the Commonwealth War Graves Commission website was Gerald Leslie Hardwick, who was also killed during the war. Gerald was a private (15040) in the Canadian Corps Cavalry and was killed in action on 26 September 1916. Like Oswald he has no known grave and his name is commemorated on the Vimy Memorial. According to ancestry.co.uk, Emma married Frederick Hardwick in 1880. The couple are recorded on the 1881 census as being Mr and Mrs Hardwick. Ten years later, on the 1891 census, I could find no record of Frederick, and Emma is shown under her maiden name of Farmer living with her parents and four brothers and sisters. It is definitely the same person as she is shown as having a son, Reginald William Hardwick, but there is no record of her having a son by the name of Gerald Leslie Hardwick.

F. Hills. There are twenty-five men listed on the Commonwealth War Graves Commission website with the same initial and surname. One of these men, Frederick Mervyn Hills, had parents Edward and Eliza Hills whose address was Lenworth, Maidstone. He had won a scholarship to Maidstone Grammar School before going on to become a civil engineer. He was 34 years of age and a second lieutenant in the 3rd Battalion (attached to the 2nd Battalion), Northamptonshire Regiment, when he was killed in action on 27 July 1917 after a German artillery shell struck the building he was in. Records held by Maidstone Grammar School indicate that he was also deployed as an intelligence officer as well as being in charge of a Lewis Gun unit. He is buried at the Perth Cemetery, China Wall, West-Vlaanderen.

Although recorded on the school's Roll of Honour as C. Hobson, it would appear that this refers to Robert Carl Hobson, who was known by his second name of Carl. Although the Commonwealth War Graves Commission website records his name as Robert Charles, the 1901 census shows him as Carl R. Hobson, who was a pupil at Maidstone Grammar School between 1901 and 1903. Robert had two brothers: Bernard Dalby Hobson who was five years his senior, and Harold who was nine years older. With the outbreak of the war Robert, who had previously served as an officer in the 1st Battalion, Home Counties Field Artillery, for six years, but resigned his commission in 1910, joined up and eventually became a captain in the 12th Battalion, Northumberland Fusiliers, and was without question a very brave man, having previously been mentioned in despatches and awarded the Military Cross and Bar, one of the awards being given when he volunteered to remain in a forward position so as to be able to provide up-to-date intelligence reports on the Germans. He was wounded during fighting at Vimy Ridge and sent back to England for treatment where he spent time at the Hyde Park Military Hospital at Plymouth. Sadly, at the age of 31, he died the day before the signing of the Armistice, on 10 November 1918, of pleurisy and peritonitis. He was buried in Plymouth's Efford Cemetery.

Robert Hobson's brother Bernard enlisted on 3 December 1915, at Piccadilly in London and became private 10148 in the 4th/1st Home Counties Field Ambulance. He was 32 years of age and a married man whose home was then at 10 King Edward Road, Rochester. Initially he was placed on the Army Reserve until he was mobilized on 4 May 1916. He never served abroad, spending his years on the home front until he was placed on the Army Reserve on 9 April 1919 before being demobilized on 31 March 1920 having served for a total of 4 years and 120 days. He was promoted to the rank of corporal on 30 December 1916 when his service number changed to 10162.

George Bertram Pollock Hodsoll was 39 years of age and a captain in the 3rd Battalion, (Special Reserve) Suffolk Regiment. After attending Maidstone Grammar School between 1885 and 1893, where he was a keen sportsman, he went up to University College, Oxford. He later obtained a commission as a second lieutenant in the Cambridgeshire Militia, then the 4th Battalion, Suffolk Regiment, in December 1902

G.B.P. Hodsoll.

before ending up in the 3rd Battalion of the same regiment with whom he became a company commander on 5 August 1914. He arrived in France on 23 October and was attached to the 1st Battalion, Cheshire Regiment. He was killed in action on 7 November 1914 while bravely leading his men in a counter-attack during fighting at the First Battle of Ypres. The regiment's adjutant, Captain L. Frost, wrote the following in a letter to George's wife Olive, whom he had married on 1 June 1914 in Edinburgh:

> *On 7 Nov. about three o'clock in the afternoon, the regt. on our left fell back and the Germans came through their trenches, so Capt. Hodsoll, Mr Anderson and myself, with the support of our regt. made a counter attack. Your husband had not gone more than 100 yards when he, poor fellow, was killed, he died instantaneously and could not have suffered any pain at all. He died giving his life for his country at a very critical moment, if this counter attack had failed, it would have meant the whole line coming back. He died a glorious and magnificent death.*

His body was recovered and he was buried the same evening close to where he died in a wood near a chateau which was about three miles east of Ypres. A wooden cross with his name on it was placed on the grave. Sadly, the location of his grave was lost and his name was subsequently commemorated on the Ypres, Menin Gate, memorial. He was a keen sportsman, especially football, at which he excelled. He represented the Casuals and the Corinthians, touring with both teams on the continent and in South Africa. He had also captained the Army's football team on several occasions.

Duncan McPherson Studdert Holmes was 26 years of age and a second lieutenant in the 9th Battalion, Cheshire Regiment, when, it is believed, he was killed in action on 4 March 1916 while out on a listening patrol at what was referred to as the Boar's Head, at Richebourg. His body was never recovered. He has no known grave and his name is commemorated on the Loos Memorial. His father, Richard Holmes, had died in Maidstone in 1899, and his mother died in Wolverhampton on 14 July 1915.

Frank Neville Johnson was 21 years of age, having been born in Maidstone in 1896, and a sergeant (G/53016) in the 32nd Battalion, Royal Fusiliers (London Regiment), and a holder of the Military Medal, when he died of his wounds on the Western Front on 22 June 1917. He is buried at the Étaples Military Cemetery which is in the Pas-de-Calais. His parents, Frederick and Amy, lived at 8 Albion Place in Maidstone with their three daughters, Norah, Monica and Joyce, and their elder son Leslie. Even though Frederick was only a clerk at a paper manufacturer's, the family was still affluent enough to have a servant, 21-year-old Edith Esther Elizabeth Yorke.

F.N. Johnson.

Donald Montgomery Johnston was 39 years of age and a private (25219) in the 1st Battalion, Grenadier Guards, when he died of nephritis – inflammation of the kidneys – on 7 February 1917. He is buried at the Grove Town Cemetery in Méaulte in the Somme. Prior to going off to war he was still living with his parents, John and Sarah Johnston, at 30 Upper Fant Road, Maidstone.

Gordon Black Johnston was born in Maidstone in 1884, but before the war was living at 4 Bath Street, Brighton, Sussex, where he was a bank clerk. During the war he became a lieutenant in the 1st/4th Battalion, Royal Sussex Regiment, and died at 35 years of age on 22 October 1918 while

G.B. Johnston.

serving in Mesopotamia. He is buried at the Baghdad North Gate Cemetery. He was Donald's younger brother.

There was another brother, Duncan Matheson Johnston, who was the eldest of the three boys, he survived the war having served as a private (205396) in the Royal Scots Fusiliers during the First World War.

Merthyr Laurence had been a pupil at Maidstone Grammar School between 1907 and 1910. With the outbreak of war he enlisted in the Army. He was 21 years of age and a sergeant (M2/188540) in 'Y' Siege Park, attached to XXII Corps, Heavy Artillery, Royal Army Service Corps, when he was killed in an accident on 16 March 1919. He is buried at the Valenciennes St. Roch Communal Cemetery, Nord, France. His parents, Frank and Gertrude Laurence, lived at Hope Cottage, Maidstone, Kent.

Stuart Laurence was the older brother of Merthyr by some six years. He was a second lieutenant in the 10th (Kent County) Battalion, Queen's Own (Royal West Kent Regiment), when he was killed in action at the Battle of Flers-Courcelette on 17 September 1916; he was 24 years of age. The 10th Battalion was raised on 3 May 1915 at Maidstone at the request of the Army Council by Lord Harris, who was the Vice-Lieutenant of Kent. They underwent their basic training near Maidstone before moving on to Aldershot for final training in January 1916. They arrived in France four months later on 4 May, initially settling in the areas of Hazebrouck and Bailleul. Stuart is buried at the Bernafay Wood British Cemetery at Montauban in the Somme.

John Brice Matthews was a pupil at Maidstone Grammar School between 1908 and 1914. Before the war he had been a sergeant in the Maidstone Officer Training Corps. At the outbreak of the war he was still only 17 years of age but left school to enlist and, at 19 years of age, he had already been promoted to the rank of captain with the 7th Battalion, Queen's Own (Royal West Kent) Regiment. At six feet four inches he was extremely tall, even by today's standards. He was killed in action during fighting on the Western Front in France and is buried at the Regina Trench Cemetery, Grandcourt, in the Somme. The family home was the School House, Hartlesham, near Maidstone, where

J.B. Matthews.

John's parents – John senior, who was a schoolmaster, and his mother Kate – and their daughter Kathleen all lived.

William McVicar was a lieutenant and a quartermaster in the Machine Gun Corps. He had served in the South African campaign during the Second Boer War, as well as in Ireland, India, Malta and Singapore, and been awarded the Army's Long Service and Good Conduct Medal. He died aged 43 on 17 July 1919 of a hemorrhage of the lungs while still a serving soldier. He is buried at the Grantham Cemetery in Lincolnshire. His parents, Robert and Anne McVicar, lived in the High Street, Maidstone.

W. McVicar.

Henry Edward Mercer was a pupil at the Maidstone Grammar School between 1910 and 1911, he was also a native of Maidstone. He enlisted in the early part of the war and became a private (200373) in the 3rd/4th Battalion, Queen's Own (Royal West Kent Regiment). He was 20 years of age when he died on 11 November 1917 and is buried at the Talana Farm Cemetery in West-Vlaanderen, Belgium. Before the war his parents, Edward and Florence Mercer, lived at 51 John Street in Maidstone along with their other son Victor, their two daughters, Olive and Rosetta, and 78-year-old Charles Whitehead who lodged with them.

Stanley Arthur Meyers had been a pupil at Maidstone Grammar School between 1901 and 1903. After the outbreak of the war he received a commission as a second lieutenant in the 1st (City of London) Battalion, London Regiment (Royal Fusiliers), who he was serving with when he was killed on 26 October 1917 aged 32. He has no known grave and his name is commemorated on the Tyne Cot Memorial. Before the war he lived with his parents, Barnett and Eliza Meyers, his sister Dorothy, and a servant by the name of Winifred Ralph, at 45 Hastings Road, Maidstone.

Howard Lester Millen had attended Maidstone Grammar School between 1894 and 1897. He was 37 years of age and a private (G/38336) in the 16th (Home Service) Battalion, the Queen's Own (Royal West Surrey Regiment), when he died on 27 January 1917 at the Connaught Hospital in Aldershot. He is buried at Maidstone Cemetery. He had previously served as a private (15686) with the Royal West Kent Regiment. The Commonwealth War Graves Commission website records him as being Harold Lester Millen, but the handwritten sheet of the 1911 census clearly shows Howard rather than Harold, and this is definitely the same man. He must have been either wounded or contracted an illness such as pneumonia and returned home for medical treatment. Before the war he was an assistant hairdresser and lived with his parents Benjamin and Alma Millen and his younger brother Leslie at 4 Middle Row, 103 High Street, Maidstone. He had six other brothers and sisters who had all left home before the outbreak of the war.

Frederick John Moseley had been a pupil at the Maidstone Grammar School between 1909 and 1913. He enlisted early in the war and was eventually promoted to the rank of corporal (G/23850) in the 6th Battalion, Queen's Own (Royal West Kent Regiment). He was awarded the Military Medal for his bravery in the face of the enemy at Vimy Ridge and was 20 when he was killed in action on 1 July 1918. He is buried at the Bouzincourt Ridge Cemetery at Albert, Somme, France. His parents Rodney and Harriet Moseley lived at 127 Union Street, Maidstone.

Another son, Harold Rubinstein Mosely, who at the time of his enlistment on 5 September 1914 at Maidstone was living at 59 John Street, arrived in Egypt on 7 October 1915. Before the war was at an end, he had served with three different regiments. He was a private (1181) in the 1st/1 Battalion, West Kent Yeomanry, a sapper (233845) in the Royal Engineers, and a private (270723) in the 10th Battalion, East Kent Regiment, before being finally demobilized on 13 June 1919. An interesting entry on his Army service record said the following:

Transferred to Royal Engineers (TF) as Pioneer with effect from 3/4/17 and posted to the Pigeon Section RE, EEF, with effect from 4/4/17.

The family's second youngest son, Leonard James Moseley, served in the Royal Navy as an able seaman second class. He enlisted on 28

February 1918 just after his 18th birthday, with his last day of service being just over a month later on 31 March.

The eldest son was Robert George Moseley who at the start of the war was 29 years of age. He was a private (437) in the 1st Battalion, Queen's Own (Royal West Kent Regiment). He arrived in France at Le Havre on 15 August 1914 and died of his wounds on 24 April 1915. Here is an entry from the war diary of the 1st Battalion Queen's Own (Royal West Kent Regiment) for 24 April 1915:

At 1pm an urgent message was received that the battalion was to move back again at once to the canal bank here to be in support as it was reported the Canadian Division was being hard pressed.

Here the battalion remained until dusk when it took up an entrenched position on the west side of the canal. All afternoon the French had been attacking and had been gaining ground slowly.

Their method was to make short advances of about 1000 yards and there dig trenches preparatory to making a further advance.

The night was very wet and was spent by the battalion on the canal bank.

The entry is noticeable for there being no record of any of the battalion having been wounded or dying on that day. Robert was buried at the Poperinghe Old Military Cemetery, West Vlaanderen, Belgium.

Henry Robert Mount attended Maidstone Grammar School for two years between 1909 and 1911, having won a Blue Coat scholarship to get there. While at the school he lodged with the Twist family who lived at 2 Upper Stone Street, Wrens Cross, Maidstone, which was the home of local police constable Arthur Thomas Twist and his family. Henry's own father, also Henry, was a police sergeant with the Kent Constabulary stationed at Deal. After finishing his education he went to work for the Post Office, enlisting soon after the outbreak of war on 24 November 1914 as a Sapper (1208) with the 28th Home Counties

Division Signal Company, of the Royal Engineers. He arrived in France on 15 January 1915 and four months later was killed in action, on 8 May 1915. He has no known grave and his name is commemorated on the Ypres Menin Gate Memorial. His name is also recorded on the Maidstone Post Office Roll of Honour.

J.W. Parks.

John Wynard Parks had been a pupil at Maidstone Grammar School between 1907 and 1909. He was 24 years of age and a captain in the 1st Battalion, East Lancashire Regiment, when he was wounded in action during April 1917 at Gavrelle in France. It would be nearly two and a half years before he would die from his wounds on 12 August 1919 at Queen's Hospital in Sidcup which at the time specialized in performing plastic surgery of the face. He is buried at the Chislehurst Cemetery in Kent. He had previously been mentioned in despatches and awarded the Military Cross for acts of bravery.

Percy Robinson was a pupil at Maidstone Grammar School for three years between 1893 and 1896. After completing his education he went to work in the brewery industry becoming a clerk. Before the war he was lodging at 38 King Edward Road, Maidstone, with a Mrs Henrietta Stannard. Percy's younger brother Leonard also lodged there. Percy had four brothers and four sisters. With the outbreak of war, and Percy already 34 years of age, he enlisted and became a private (PS/10307) in the 8th Battalion, Royal Fusiliers. He was killed in action on 7 October 1916. His name is commemorated on the Thiepval Memorial.

His youngest brother James Robinson has an interesting story. He enlisted in the Royal Marines Light Infantry on 13 March 1900 as private 11473. He appears on the 1911 census, but on 22 April 1915 he emigrated to Canada and enlisted in the Canadian Overseas Expeditionary Force under the alias of Robert Fenwick. Why an alias and why that particular name are questions I do not have the answers to. As best as I have been able to discover, James or rather Robert, survived the war.

James Lawrence Cathcart Sutherland had been a pupil at Maidstone for six years between 1909 and 1915 after winning the Robert James Worsley Scholarship. When he was 20 years of age he was a lieutenant in the Royal West Kent Regiment attached to 104 Squadron Royal Air Force. His attachment must have been before 1 April 1918 as initially he had also served with the Royal Flying Corps. He died of a wound to one of his legs which he received in action on 19 August 1918. He had been awarded the Military Cross. He is buried at the Chambieres French National Cemetery which is at Metz in the Moselle. When his wartime service medals were issued in early 1922 they were sent to C.C. Sutherland Esq. c/o Ellis & Ellis, 35 Earl Street, Maidstone, Kent.

Garrett Saveall spent five years as a pupil at Maidstone Grammar School between 1905 and 1910, having won a scholarship to get there. After leaving school he became a clerk at a local brewery. The family had fallen on hard times. Garrett's father William had lost his job as a corn dealer by the time of the 1911 census. The family home at Ware Street, Thurnham, Mount Pleasant, Bearsted, must have been substantial as they had let part of it out to Albert Wallace Grant, his wife, their three young children and Eleanor Simpson, who was the Grant children's governess. When the war came Garrett received a commission as a second lieutenant with the 7th Battalion, Queen's Own (Royal West Kent Regiment). He was killed in action during the fighting at Trônes Wood on 13 July 1916 at the Battle of the Somme. His body was never recovered, and accordingly his name is commemorated on the Thiepval Memorial. He was 21 years of age. After the war his parents, William and Edith Saveall, had moved to The Hermitage, Boxley, Maidstone.

Arthur Frederick Tong had been a pupil at Maidstone Grammar School between 1909 and 1915 and was only 16 years of age at the outbreak of the war. When he enlisted he decided he wanted to be a flyer and so joined the Royal Flying Corps and became a lieutenant in 217 Squadron. On 1 April 1918 the Royal Flying Corps became part of the newly formed Royal Air Force. On 28 September 1918, when he was 20 years of age, he was in an Airco DH4 Bomber aircraft on a raid over German lines near Dunkirk when he was shot down and killed. He is buried at the Croix-Rouge Military Cemetery at

Quaedypre, Nord, France. His parents, Arthur and Ellen Tong, lived at a house on East Street, Harrietsham, Maidstone.

H. Tupper.

Harold Tupper was a pupil at Maidstone Grammar School between 1906 and 1910 where, besides other achievements, he was the captain of the football and cricket elevens. He was 26 years of age and a lieutenant in the Royal Fusiliers when he died of meningitis after being operated on for a head wound at the Royal Infirmary Hospital in Manchester on 22 July 1918. He had suffered wounds during fighting at Bazentin-le-Petit on 4 August 1916. He is buried in the cemetery of St. John the Baptist Church in Harrietsham. According to the 1911 census the family home was The Roebuck Inn, West Street, Hartlesham, where his father Thomas was the landlord and his wife Mary helped behind the bar. Harold also had an elder sister, Hilda, who like her mother helped behind the bar. After the war Harold's parents had moved to a house named Bowness in Hartlesham.

Edward Henry Tolhurst was a pupil at Maidstone Grammar School between 1908 and 1911. After the outbreak of war he enlisted and became a private (5026) in the 15th Battalion, London Regiment (Prince of Wales Own Civil Service Rifles). Sadly he was killed in action on 14 August 1916 when he was still only 19 years of age. He is buried in the Maroeuil British Cemetery in the Pas-de-Calais. He lived with his parents, Edward and Louisa Tolhurst, and his younger brother Herbert at 31 Pudding Lane, Maidstone, although after the war his parents moved to 119 Union Street.

J.L. Warry.

John Lucas Warry, known as Jack, was born in Woolwich, Kent in 1885 and attended Maidstone Grammar School for two years between 1896 and 1898, where he captained the cricket team in his first year. Before the war he was an architect and lived at 8 Colehill Gardens, Fulham Palace Road in south west London with his wife Winifred. With the coming of the war he enlisted as a private (3633) in the 28th Battalion, London Regiment. He later gained a commission and rose to the rank of captain with the 8th Battalion, Sherwood Foresters (Notts & Derby Regiment). He was killed in action leading his men 'over the top' near St. Quentin on 27 April 1917. He is buried in the Peronne Communal Cemetery Extension in the Somme. Both of the regiments John served with were Territorial units.

Henry Richard Waterman was a pupil at Maidstone Grammar School between 1907 and 1914 but did not finish his education; instead he joined up to go and serve King and country. He was commissioned as a lieutenant in the 3rd Battalion, Middlesex Regiment, after having passed out of Sandhurst Military College. He first arrived in France on 13 April 1916 and just four months later, on 28 August, was killed in action. He is buried at the Serre Road No. 2 Cemetery in the Somme. Henry was born in Maidstone in 1898 and before the war was living at 12 College Road, Maidstone, with his parents Edward and Helen and his two younger sisters, Molly and Betty. When Mrs Waterman applied for her son's wartime campaign medals on 4 February 1922 she was then living at 98 Mill Street, Maidstone.

Dudley Francis Small was a pupil at Maidstone Grammar School between 1897 and 1901. Before the war Dudley was living with his parents and younger brother Howard at Hill House in East Fairleigh. He was a dentist by profession, which made it somewhat strange that he wasn't directed towards the Royal Army Medical Corps where his skills would have been greatly appreciated. Dudley had a younger brother Howard who I could find no trace of having served during the war, but whether or not he did, he survived and lived to be 80 years of age, passing away in 1970 in Maidstone. Dudley was commissioned in to the 15th Battalion, Cheshire Regiment, and was later promoted to the rank of captain. He was killed in action on 24 March 1918 and has no known grave, but his name is commemorated on the Pozières Memorial.

George Ormrod wasn't an ex-pupil, he was an ex-master of Maidstone Grammar school, having left his job to go off and fight in the war. He became a lieutenant in the 5th Battalion, Royal Sussex Regiment, and was killed in action on 18 September 1918. Prior to receiving his commission, George had been a private (4203) in the same regiment. Before the war George had lived at 17 Hastings Road in Maidstone. After his death his widow moved to Great Missenden in Buckinghamshire. He is buried at the Cerisy-Gailly Military Cemetery in the Somme.

Maidstone Prison

One of the more unusual memorials to the dead of the First World War is undoubtedly the one that adorns the prison chapel at HMP Maidstone and which was erected by the then prison chaplain, the Reverend W.L. Cottrell. It is in the form of a stained glass window. The wording on it is somewhat unique and reads as follows:

> To the glory of God and in memory of those released
> from this prison who fought and fell in
> the Great War, 1914-1919

There are no names on the memorial.

Maidstone Post Office

The Post Office in Maidstone has a marble plaque in its premises at Bank Street to commemorate the names of eight members of its staff who left to go and serve their country and who sadly never returned home. The inscription on the plaque is as follows:

> Erected by the Maidstone District Post Office staff
> in memory and honour of their colleagues who laid down
> their lives in the Great War
> 1914-1919

> Private L/6506 Frank Moody
> Sapper 1208 Henry Robert Mount
> Rifleman 565059 George Meek
> Private 225656 Richard William Black
> Sapper 191478 Ernest Edward Froud
> Private 325084 James Thomas Robinson
> Private T/240093 William George Maytum
> Lance Corporal 96373 Sydney William James Dann

Private Moody was the first man to die when he was killed on 28 October 1914. Sapper Mount died in 1915. Two more were killed in 1917: Rifleman Meek and Private Maytum. A further three died in 1918: Private Black, Sapper Froud and Private Robinson. Lance Corporal Dann was the last casualty when he died of his wounds on 24 March 1919. Before the war he had lived with his parents Sydney and Emily Dann and his younger sister Edna at 37 Hardy Street, Maidstone.

Maidstone War Memorial
The Maidstone Civic War Memorial sadly doesn't have the names of the men inscribed on it that it is there to commemorate.

Maidstone War Memorial.

The memorial was designed by Sir George Frampton and was unveiled by Lieutenant Colonel Cornwallis on 21 June 1922. It has a limestone plinth upon which sits a bronze statue of Saint George and a slain dragon. The inscription on it reads:

In honour of our glorious dead
who gave their lives in the Great War,
for ever honoured and for ever mourned.
1914-1918, 1939-1945 and in later conflicts

I don't believe there is a definitive answer as to exactly how many men there were from Maidstone who died in the First World War. This is because it depends on what criteria are used. As there are no names on the War Memorial, no criteria were ever applied to this matter. Most war memorials up and down the country do have the names of the men from their town, village or parish named on them and it was often not clear which names should be included and which should not. Having carried out a search of the Commonwealth War Graves Commission (CWGC) website of the name 'Maidstone', it throws up 910 names, and if you look on Geoff's Search Engine as part of hut-six.co.uk, which appears to have used the CWGC as its main source of information, that throws up 852, so hopefully in the list I have compiled below the number of men who were killed in or died as a result of their involvement in the First World War and who had any kind of connection with Maidstone will be as correct as it can be.

The list is in year order, with each year then being in alphabetic order. I have also included the regiment, corps, or ship:

1914

Bailey, W H	Queen's Own (Royal West Kent Regiment)
Banks, R	Queen's Own (Royal West Kent Regiment)
Buckingham, A W	Gordon Highlanders
Burgess, H W	Royal Navy (HMS *Cressy*)
Burton, G	Royal Field Artillery
Cale, T F	Lincolnshire Regiment
Chambers, E	Royal Navy (HMS *Hogue*)
Chandler, F S	Rifle Brigade
Cleggett, W J	Queen's Own (Royal West Kent Regiment)
Coe, B W	Royal Navy (HMS *Hogue*)
Copland, F	West Yorkshire Regiment (Prince of Wales Own)

Crayford, V	Royal Marine Light Infantry
Damms, A	Royal Fusiliers
Dooner, A E C T	Royal Welsh Fusiliers
Drewett, G F	Royal Marine Light Infantry
Eldridge, A	Queen's Own (Royal West Kent Regiment)
Fletcher, R S	Northumberland Fusiliers
Fosher, H	Rifle Brigade
Fuller, W	South Lancashire Regiment
Gardiner, R H	Rifle Brigade
Gilbey, C J	Queen's Own (Royal West Kent Regiment)
Grubb, W B W	Royal Navy (HMS *Cressy*)
Head, R A	6th Dragoon Guards (Carabiniers)
Hobson, G	Royal Navy (HMS *MD2*)
Hodges, W H	Queen's Own (Royal West Kent Regiment)
Hodgkin, G	Royal Australian Navy
Hoper, E S J	Royal Navy (HMS *Hawke*)
Johnson, F	Bedfordshire Regiment
Jones, J R	Royal Marine Light Infantry
Jones, R E	7th Dragoon Guards (Princess Royal's)
Knight, A A	Royal Navy (HMS *Pathfinder*)
Kemp, A G	Canadian Infantry
Marshall, E F	Royal Engineers
McStay, T G	King's Royal Rifle Corps
Mott, G	Royal Navy (HMS *Hogue*)
Penfold, G H	Royal Navy (HMS *Hawke*)
Penney, W H	Queen's Own (Royal West Kent Regiment)
Pollock-Hodsoll, G B	Suffolk Regiment
Potter, B C	Royal Navy (HMS *Aboukir*)
Ray, W E	Royal Engineers
Relf, E A	Leicestershire Regiment
Rose, C E	Royal Marine Light Infantry
Sage, A	Queen's Own (Royal West Kent Regiment)
Scarlett, L F	Royal Australian Navy
Slater, W J	Royal Naval Reserve (HM *Drifter Eyrie*)
Solman, H	Royal Navy (HMS *King Edward Vll*)
Standing, G W	Royal Navy (HMS *Pathfinder*)

Sturmer, A	The Buffs (East Kent Regiment)
Styance, A	Royal Navy (HMS *Cressy*)
Vanson, A J	1st (Royal) Dragoons
Walliker, A H	East Surrey Regiment
Waters, W G	12th (Prince of Wales Royal) Lancers
Watts, R W	The Buffs (East Kent Regiment)
Wood, A A	Grenadier Guards
Woods, J T	1st Life Guards
Wright, T	The Buffs (East Kent Regiment)

1915

Ames, W	Queen's Own (Royal West Kent Regiment)
Baker, H	The Buffs (East Kent Regiment)
Ballard, S G	London Regiment (City of London Rifles)
Barden, G I G	Queen's Own (Royal West Kent Regiment)
Bennett, R H	Royal Army Medical Corps
Bloomfield, H	Royal Navy (HMS *Natal*)
Boorman, A E	Queen's Own (Royal West Kent Regiment)
Brunger, A W	Queen's Own (Royal West Kent Regiment)
Bryant, C	Royal Navy (HMS *Formidable*)
Burrluck, H	The Queen's (Royal West Surrey Regiment)
Butcher, C E	Grenadier Guards
Butcher, J	The Buffs (East Kent Regiment)
Carpenter, J	Canadian Infantry
Casswell, R	Somerset Light Infantry
Chambers, H W	Queen's Own (Royal West Kent Regiment)
Chapman, P C	Royal Artillery
Cheeseman, G	Royal Engineers
Childs, P G	Royal Sussex Regiment
Chittenden, S	Royal Marine Light Infantry
Clark, F	Royal Marine Light Infantry
Clifthill, G	York and Lancaster Regiment
Coatsworth, E	Royal Sussex Regiment
Cole, J I	Royal Marine Light Infantry
Coleman, E J	Royal Navy (HMS *ME20*)
Curtis, F W	Queen's Own (Royal West Kent Regiment)

Dadson, F	Royal Engineers
Danes, A W	The Buffs (East Kent Regiment)
Denman, F	Queen's Own (Royal West Kent Regiment)
Diplock, R R	East Yorkshire Regiment
Doughty, F	Royal Field Artillery
Edmett, G	King's Shropshire Light Infantry
Eley, L F	Wiltshire Regiment
Eley, W R	Duke of Cornwall's Light Infantry
Excell, A	Royal Warwickshire Regiment
Fairow, C W	The Buffs (East Kent Regiment)
Farrow, W	Devonshire Regiment
Feaver, H O	The Queen's (Royal West Surrey Regiment)
Ferguson, R	Otago Regiment NZEF
Ford, A	Royal Army Medical Corps
Fowler, A J	Queen's Own (Royal West Kent Regiment)
Francis, W W	The Buffs (East Kent Regiment)
Freeman, R W	Queen's Own (Royal West Kent Regiment)
Golden, J	Royal Navy (HMS *Princess Irene*)
Golding, T A	The Buffs (East Kent Regiment)
Goldsmith, B H	The Buffs (East Kent Regiment)
Goodsell, P	Royal Sussex Regiment
Goodwin, C W	Royal Navy (HMS *India*)
Griffiths, L	Queen's Own (Royal West Kent Regiment)
Haisman, N A	Royal Navy (HMS *Formidable*)
Harman, H	Queen's Own (Royal West Kent Regiment)
Hart, E	Norfolk Regiment
Hatter, C E	The Buffs (East Kent Regiment)
Hearn, G	Royal Navy (HMS *Princess Irene*)
Hedge, H	Queen's Own (Royal West Kent Regiment)
Heron, W	The Queen's (Royal West Surrey Regiment)
Hoile, A W	Royal Field Artillery
Hollamby, A E	Canadian Infantry
Holmes, G W V	The Buffs (East Kent Regiment)
Ingram, L	The Buffs (East Kent Regiment)
Inwood, G	Royal Garrison Artillery
Jones, A	Hampshire Regiment

Josey, R	Royal Engineers
Jukes, A	Coldstream Guards
Lambden, G	Canadian Infantry
Lampkin, G P	Royal Engineers
Longhurst, H J	Royal Engineers
Longhurst, P	Worcestershire Regiment
Mapp, J	Queen's Own (Royal West Kent Regiment)
Marchant, W E	Royal Fusiliers
Martin, C	Welsh Regiment
Martin, S J	Canadian Infantry
McLean, A	The Buffs (East Kent Regiment)
Mitchell, E	Worcestershire Regiment
Morland, W H	Royal Scots
Moseley, R G	Queen's Own (Royal West Kent Regiment)
Mullins, E J	Royal Engineers
Mullins, S H	Royal Engineers
Murrell, A J	The Buffs (East Kent Regiment)
Neale, A	Canadian Infantry
Newman, T W	Hampshire Regiment
Norris, W A	Royal Scots
North, A W	The Buffs (East Kent Regiment)
Oliver, G H	South Wales Borderers
Osborne, C R	Queen's Own (Royal West Kent Regiment)
Page, L J	Queen's Own (Royal West Kent Regiment)
Parks, G	Queen's own (Royal West Kent Regiment)
Pearson, J W	Royal Warwickshire Regiment
Perrin, G H	Royal Field Artillery
Pettifer, H	The Buffs (East Kent Regiment)
Pierson, R	Essex Regiment
Poole, J	The Buffs (East Kent Regiment)
Prentis, O J	Royal Navy (HMS *Wolverine*)
Purrott, J E A	Royal Field Artillery
Randall, A E	York & Lancaster Regiment
Randall, T A	Queen's Own (Royal West Kent Regiment)
Richardson, E L	Bedfordshire Regiment
Ruby, J	Queen's Own (Royal West Kent Regiment)

Saunders, F	Royal Sussex Regiment
Seager, J O	Royal Navy (HMS *Vivid*)
Sharp, F	Queen's Own (Royal West Kent Regiment)
Sheehan, C T	Royal Navy (HMS *Swiftsure*)
Shields, A	Queen's Own (Royal West Kent Regiment)
Simmonds, W G	Queen's Own (Royal West Kent Regiment)
Smith, A T J	The Buffs (East Kent Regiment)
Smith, W T	Royal Navy (HMS *Wildfire*)
Stevens, A S	The Buffs (East Kent Regiment)
Stevens, O	Royal Army Medical Corps
Summers, W A	The Queen's (Royal West Surrey Regiment)
Tanton, J H	Royal Field Artillery
Taylor, G	Royal Engineers
Townsend, T	The Buffs (East Kent Regiment)
Tupper, C E	The Buffs (East Kent Regiment)
Veitch, G A	The Buffs (East Kent Regiment)
Veitch, W J	Royal Field Artillery
Walkey, C A	London Regiment
Weedon, S C	Queen's Own (Royal West Kent Regiment)
Wickens, F	Queen's Own (Royal West Kent Regiment)
Winch, R B	The Buffs (East Kent Regiment)
Winchester, P T	Worcestershire Regiment
Wood, W J	Canadian Infantry
Wycherley, B W	Monmouthshire Regiment

1916

Adams, F	Queen's Own (Royal West Kent Regiment)
Aiston, R G	Royal Army Ordnance Corps
Allcorn, T L	Queen's Own (Royal West Kent Regiment)
Allmen, G A	Queen's Own (Royal West Kent Regiment)
Ashby, H E	The Buffs (East Kent Regiment)
Baker, F J	Royal Garrison Artillery
Ball, R W	Royal Navy (HMS *Indefatigable*)
Barker, C I	Queen's Own (Royal West Kent Regiment)
Barton, A H	Royal Warwickshire Regiment
Beard, J T R	Royal Engineers

Bingham, J G	Royal Field Artillery
Blackman, P R	Middlesex Regiment
Britter, J J	Royal Field Artillery
Bromley, H	Royal Field Artillery
Brook, W	Queen's Own (Royal West Kent Regiment)
Brooks, F	London Regiment
Broomfield, J	East Surrey Regiment
Brown, A W	Royal Army Medical Corps
Brown, C W	Queen's Own (Royal West Kent Regiment)
Brown, P A	Royal Army Medical Corps
Buck, A	Royal Fusiliers
Buckingham, E J	Royal Fusiliers
Burr, H D	Grenadier Guards
Calder, T	Canadian Infantry
Carter, C	Welsh Guards
Cathcart, D A	Queen's Own (Royal West Kent Regiment)
Chambers, J	King's Royal Rifle Corps
Chambers, W J	East Surrey Regiment
Champion, C E	Queen's Own (Royal West Kent Regiment)
Chapman, E P	Royal Navy (HMS *Indefatigable*)
Chapman, H	Queen's Own (Royal West Kent Regiment)
Chapman, M	West Kent Yeomanry (Queen's Own)
Cheeseman, E	Queen's Own (Royal West Kent Regiment)
Chevous, S G	The Buffs (East Kent Regiment)
Chittenden, J D	Army Service Corps
Clegg, T	Queen's Own (Royal West Kent Regiment)
Collison, A	Queen's Own (Royal West Kent Regiment)
Cook, C	Queen's Own (Royal West Kent Regiment)
Cook, G	Queen's Own (Royal West Kent Regiment)
Cook, J	Queen's Own (Royal West Kent Regiment)
Coppins, G E	Queen's Own (Royal West Kent Regiment)
Cottenham, C A	Queen's Own (Royal West Kent Regiment)
Cousens, W G	Queen's Own (Royal West Kent Regiment)
Crowhurst, J	The Queen's (Royal West Surrey Regiment)
Crump, W H	Royal Garrison Artillery
Culling, G	Royal Engineers

Curtis, H	Yorkshire Regiment
Davis, W J	Northumberland Fusiliers
Day, W A	Royal Field Artillery
Diprose, A H	Queen's Own (Royal West Kent Regiment)
Dixon, T	Queen's Own (Royal West Kent Regiment)
Dudley, W J	Royal Navy (HMS *Drifter Morning Star*)
Edmett, F	Machine Gun Corps (Infantry)
Everist, J H	Queen's Own (Royal West Kent Regiment)
Fagg, J R	West Kent Yeomanry (Queen's Own)
Fever, J H	Royal Navy (HMS *Indefatigable*)
Filmer, R M	Grenadier Guards
Foreman, O	King's Royal Rifle Corps
Foster, F	Queen's Own (Royal West Kent Regiment)
Fuller, H W	Royal Field Artillery
Galpin, F A	Queen's Own (Royal West Kent Regiment)
Gates, F S	Royal Army Medical Corps
Gatland, S	Queen's Own (Royal West Kent Regiment)
Gibbs, J P	Royal Marine Light Infantry
Gibson, J S	Bedfordshire Regiment
Gilbert, G	The Buffs (East Kent Regiment)
Green, F	The Buffs (East Kent Regiment)
Grey, W E G	Queen's Own (Royal West Kent Regiment)
Ground, J K	Queen's Own (Royal West Kent Regiment)
Hall, S R	Royal Engineers
Hanford, B	Canadian Infantry
Hearnden, F G	Queen's Own (Royal West Kent Regiment)
Herbert, A T	Duke of Cornwall's Light Infantry
Hibbin, R	Royal Naval Volunteer Reserve
Hills, W	Queen's Own (Royal West Kent Regiment)
Hollands, E	The Buffs (East Kent Regiment)
Hollis, W F	London Regiment (City of London Rifles)
Holmden, T J	Queen's Own (Royal West Kent Regiment)
Holmes, D M S	Cheshire Regiment
Howlett, C W	King's Own Yorkshire Light Infantry
Hughes, B L	Durham Light Infantry
Humphrey, P A	The King's (Liverpool Regiment)

Humphrey, W F	Royal Navy (HMS *Powerful*)
Hurven, J E	Queen's Own (Royal West Kent Regiment)
Jeffrey, F	Queen's Own (Royal West Kent Regiment)
Jenner, A	Queen's Own (Royal West Kent Regiment)
Joiner, J	Royal Engineers
Joyce, F R	Royal Fusiliers
Kemp, C H	Queen's Own (Royal West Kent Regiment)
Kennard, W A	Machine Gun Corps
Kenyon, P	York & Lancaster Regiment
King, A V	Middlesex Regiment
Knight, C R	Queen's Own (Royal West Kent Regiment)
Lacey, L E	Queen's Own (Royal West Kent Regiment)
Lamb, A	Essex Regiment
Latter, A J	London Regiment
Laurence, S	Queen's Own (Royal West Kent Regiment)
Lavender, C J	Queen's Own (Royal West Kent Regiment)
Leigh, J C T	The Buffs (East Kent Regiment)
Lofts, H	Royal Field Artillery
Lott, A T	Royal Army Medical Corps
Lowe, S	Queen's Own (Royal West Kent Regiment)
Lucas, C	North Staffordshire Regiment
Luck, A E	West Kent Yeomanry (Queen's Own)
Lushington, C H G	Worcestershire Regiment
Macheldon, G	The Buffs (East Kent Regiment)
Mackelden, V A	Queen's Own (Royal West Kent Regiment)
Marchant, A A	London Regiment
Marchant, R H	East Surrey Regiment
Martin, T J	The Buffs (East Kent Regiment)
Martin, J L	The Buffs (East Kent Regiment)
Martin, R D	Grenadier Guards
Maskell, T J	London Regiment (Royal Fusiliers)
Masters, F	Royal Field Artillery
Matthews, E	Queen's Own (Royal West Kent Regiment)
Mills, F	Middlesex Regiment
Mitchell, A	The Buffs (East Kent Regiment)
Mitchell, F W	Royal Field Artillery

Morris, E J	Queen's Own (Royal West Kent Regiment)
Nuttall, J L	Welsh Regiment
Orman, A	Royal Garrison Artillery
Packman, T A	Royal Horse Artillery
Parrett, W H	Royal Garrison Artillery
Pearman, G A	Queen's Own (Royal West Kent Regiment)
Pearson, C E	Rifle Brigade
Perriman, H	The Buffs (East Kent Regiment)
Pink, D S	Queen's Own (Royal West Kent Regiment)
Potter, F	Worcestershire Regiment
Pratt, P G	Middlesex Regiment
Pudney, B H	Royal Berkshire Regiment
Pullen, F	Canadian Infantry
Rabey, W T	Queen's Own (Royal West Kent Regiment)
Relf, E F	Queen's Own (Royal West Kent Regiment)
Relf, L	Oxford & Bucks Light Infantry
Richards, A E	Royal Field Artillery
Roberts, J S	Grenadier Guards
Robinson, A S	Grenadier Guards
Robinson, P	Royal Fusiliers
Roe, J B O	Canadian Infantry
Rouse, A C	Worcestershire Regiment
Sandell, C	Middlesex Regiment
Saunders, B	The Buffs (East Kent Regiment)
Saveall, G	Queen's Own (Royal West Kent Regiment)
Sawkins, E A	Queen's Own (Royal West Kent Regiment)
Seager, G W	Royal Scots Fusiliers
Shileds, A	Queen's Own (Royal West Kent Regiment)
Shoebridge, W J	Cheshire Regiment
Sills, W	Royal Field Artillery
Smith, A H	Queen's Own (Royal West Kent Regiment)
Smith, H D	Royal Field Artillery
Smith, L T	King's Own Yorkshire Light Infantry
Smith, S A	Somerset Light Infantry
Smith, T W	The Buffs (East Kent Regiment)
Sone, C H	Royal Army Medical Corps

Staples, S G	Queen's Own (Royal West Kent Regiment)
Stockwell, F H	Gloucestershire Regiment
Styles, J	Canadian Infantry
Swaine, H	Seaforth Highlanders
Taylor, L B	Gloucestershire Regiment
Thompson, C W	Royal Field Artillery
Thompson, H C	Middlesex Regiment
Tilby, H	Queen's Own (Royal West Kent Regiment)
Tiley, C F	Hampshire Regiment
Tiley, H	Queen's Own (Royal West Kent Regiment)
Tindall, F	Queen's Own (Royal West Kent Regiment)
Tolhurst, E H	London Reg (P of W Own Civil Service Rifles)
Towner, F J	Queen's Own (Royal West Kent Regiment)
Tree, E J	Royal Garrison Artillery
Tyman, P J	Army Service Corps
Uings, L	Queen's Own (Royal West Kent Regiment)
Underdown, F	Royal Fusiliers
Waghorne, H F	King's Own Yorkshire Light Infantry
Walkling, A	Leicestershire Regiment
Wallis, F A	Royal Sussex Regiment
Ward, A T	Queen's Own (Royal West Kent Regiment)
Waterman, H R	Middlesex Regiment
Watts, H C	Canadian Infantry
Webb, F W	Suffolk Regiment
Weller, T J	Grenadier Guards
Wenham, J	The Buffs (East Kent Regiment)
Whenham, H S	The Buffs (East Kent Regiment)
Whibley, A V	Royal Sussex Regiment
Wigan, W L	Queen's Own (Royal West Kent Regiment)
Wilding, A C	Worcestershire Regiment
Williams, E H	Queen's Own (Royal West Kent Regiment)
Winch, B J	The Buffs (East Kent Regiment)
Winchester, W A	Royal Sussex Regiment
Wintour, C J	Royal Navy (HMS *Tipperary*)
Wolfe, W	Middlesex Regiment

Wright, W	Royal Navy (HMS *Queen Mary*)
Wright, W	The Buffs (East Kent Regiment)
Young, C H A	Queen's Own (Royal West Kent Regiment)
Young, T F	Queen's Own (Royal West Kent Regiment)
Youngman, J M	East Surrey Regiment

1917

Ackland, A R	Suffolk Regiment
Ambrose, A G	London Regiment (City of London Rifles)
Andrews, R	South Lancashire Regiment
Anstey, H	Rifle Brigade
Apps, A G	Royal Navy (HMS *Vanguard*)
Apps, E J	Canadian Infantry
Apps, J H M	Northumberland Fusiliers
Apps, M	Queen's Own (Royal West Kent Regiment)
Arthur, W R	Royal Army Medical Corps
Austen, R J	Queen's Own (Royal West Kent Regiment)
Baker, A G	Royal Field Artillery
Baker, W L	Army Service Corps
Baldwin, W	Canadian Infantry
Ballard, J	The Buffs (East Kent Regiment)
Banks H P	Canadian Infantry
Barrans, A	Durham Light Infantry
Bartlett, A G	Royal Fusiliers
Baskett, M A	Queen's Own (Royal West Kent Regiment)
Batcheller, G	Royal Garrison Artillery
Beadle, S G	Middlesex Regiment
Beeby, W J	Royal Irish Rifles
Betson, J W	London Regiment
Beyer, L W	Welsh Regiment
Blackman, G W	Northumberland Fusiliers
Bodiam, E	Middlesex Regiment
Bolton, H	Grenadier Guards
Bony, S G	Queen's Own (Royal West Kent Regiment)
Boorman, G	Royal Garrison Artillery
Bottle, R E	Queen's Own (Royal West Kent Regiment)

Bottle, W	Royal Fusiliers
Bowen, J W	Royal Field Artillery
Brabant, H A	Rifle Brigade
Bradford, H T	Queen's Own (Royal West Kent Regiment)
Brann, H J	Royal Field Artillery
Bridge, A T	Army Service Corps
Bringloe, E J	Royal Sussex Regiment
Brisley, L A	Northumberland Fusiliers
Broad, G W	Machine Gun Company (Infantry)
Browning, H G	Royal Fusiliers
Buller, S J	Royal Naval Reserve (HMS *Laurentic*)
Burgess, C H	Royal Navy (HMS *Vanguard*)
Burgess, L H	Queen's Own (Royal West Kent Regiment)
Busbridge, F J	Royal Field Artillery
Butler, W W	King's Royal Rifle Corps
Carr, B R	Queen's Own (Royal West Kent Regiment)
Carr, D R	Queen's Own (Royal West Kent Regiment)
Castle, W J	Queen's Own (Royal West Kent Regiment)
Chambers, G	Middlesex Regiment
Chapman, A L	Queen's Own (Royal West Kent Regiment)
Chapman, B F	The Buffs (East Kent Regiment)
Chapman, R H	The Buffs (East Kent Regiment)
Chapman, T	Royal Engineers
Clark, A	The Buffs (East Kent Regiment)
Clarke, S M	Durham Light Infantry
Cleveland, G C	Royal Canadian Navy (HMCS *Stadacona*)
Clubbe, W H	Royal Field Artillery
Cooper, R J	Queen's Own (Royal West Kent Regiment)
Coppin, F C	Army Veterinary Corps
Cornford, E S	Canterbury Regiment NZEF
Craske, H	Royal Garrison Artillery
Culling, A W	Royal Field Artillery
Curtis, F	Welsh Guards
Diprose, H A	Queen's Own (Royal West Kent Regiment)
Dodd, R J	Royal Navy (HMS *Pembroke*)
Dovey, H	Queen's Own (Royal West Kent Regiment)

Down, T E	Royal Marine Light Infantry
Duncanson, I F	Argyle & Sutherland Highlanders
Duncanson, Miss U M	Voluntary Aid Detachment
Edmett, E G	Auckland Regiment NZEF
Edwards, W A	East Surrey Regiment
Ellis, C	British West Indies Regiment
Eveleigh, F G	Queen's Own (Royal West Kent Regiment)
Falkner, R G G	Queen's Own (Royal West Kent Regiment)
Fenwick, J	Royal Navy (HMS *Vanguard*)
Fletcher, H W	Royal Welsh Fusiliers
Fletcher, W	Rifle Brigade
Foord, E J	Queen's Own (Royal West Kent Regiment)
Ford, C T	Queen's Own (Royal West Kent Regiment)
Forster, C J	Royal Field Artillery
Froud, F G	Queen's Own (Royal West Kent Regiment)
Froud, G T	Royal Scots Fusiliers
Gardner, A J	Royal Fusiliers
Gardner, W	Royal Field Artillery
Gates, C G	Queen's Own (Royal West Kent Regiment)
Gatland, F W	Royal Garrison Artillery
Genn, H H	Rifle Brigade
Gibson, C A	Durham Light Infantry
Goodrum, W	Mercantile Marine
Gower, C	Army Service Corps
Grayham, H B	Machine Gun Corps (Infantry)
Green, S J	London Regiment (London Irish Rifles)
Grey, J G	Queen's Own (Royal West Kent Regiment)
Groom, W J	Royal Fusiliers
Gurr, J P	Queen's Own (Royal West Kent Regiment)
Gurr, W C	The Queen's (Royal West Surrey Regiment)
Hall, P H	Royal Navy (HMS *Vanguard*)
Harler, W J	Rifle Brigade
Harris, C A	North Staffordshire Regiment
Harris, J G R	Bedfordshire Regiment
Harris, R	Middlesex Regiment
Hayward, B B	Essex Regiment

Heathfield, J	West Yorkshire Regiment (Prince of Wales Own)
Hepton, G	Royal Garrison Artillery
Hepton, J F	Coldstream Guards
Hicks, J W	The Queen's (Royal West Surrey Regiment)
Higdon, F	London Regiment
Highams, T W	Queen's Own (Royal West Kent Regiment)
Hills, F M	Northamptonshire Regiment
Heselton, F	Canadian Engineers
Hodge, G	Queen's Own (Royal West Kent Regiment)
Holman, F R	London Regiment
Homewoode, M E	Queen's Own (Royal West Kent Regiment)
Honour, A E	Hampshire Regiment
Hopgood, A C	Royal Fusiliers
Horton, A E	Royal Sussex Regiment
Howe, A	Middlesex Regiment
Howes, E	London Regiment (Royal Fusiliers)
Hughes, A	Worcestershire Regiment
Hughes, A H	Royal Navy (HMS *Vanguard*)
Hughes, J S	Queen's Own (Royal West Kent Regiment)
Hyland, F H	Machine Gun Corps (Infantry)
Ingram, J	Royal Navy (HMS *Mary Rose*)
Jackson, V	The Queen's (Royal West Surrey Regiment)
Jeffrey, W E	The Queen's (Royal West Surrey Regiment)
Jenner, A	Royal Naval Air Service
Jenner, H	Royal Engineers
Jenner, P L	Army Service Corps
Johnson, F N	Royal Fusiliers
Johnston, D M	Grenadier Guards
Johnston, J	Machine Gun Corps (Infantry)
Jones, D	Canadian Infantry
Jones, J E	Royal Navy (HMS *Vanguard*)
Jordan, W E	Queen's Own (Royal West Kent Regiment)
Joy, E A	The Queen's (Royal West Surrey Regiment)
Judge, G	Royal Naval Reserve
Jury, J T	Queen's Own (Royal West Kent Regiment)

Keeley, K	Canadian Infantry
Kenshole, J	Grenadier Guards
Kimmings, H	Army Service Corps
King, C C	Royal Engineers
King, L A	Machine Gun Corps
King, R W	London Regiment (Queen Victoria Rifles)
King, S	Hertfordshire Regiment
Knight, H O	Royal Sussex Regiment
Latter, T G	Queen's Own (Royal West Kent Regiment)
Liddell, J A	Royal Garrison Artillery
Lines, G E	Royal Garrison Artillery
Link, A H	Royal Navy (HMS *Vanguard*)
Lyle, J	Gordon Highlanders
Mantle, A L	London Regiment
Marley, G R	Middlesex Regiment
Marlow, A H	Hampshire Regiment
Martin, J L	The Queen's (Royal West Surrey Regiment)
Masters, B J	Yorkshire Regiment
Matthews, J	East Surrey Regiment
Mayes, E	West Yorkshire Regiment (Prince of Wales's Own)
Mayger, F	Royal Army Medical Corps
Maytum, W G	The Buffs (East Kent Regiment)
Medhurst, S	Queen's Own (Royal West Kent Regiment)
Medhurst, W	Royal Navy
Meek, G	London Regiment (Queen's Westminster Rifles)
Mellor, R	Royal Army Medical Corps
Mepham, E J	South Wales Borderers
Mercer, H	Queen's Own (Royal West Kent Regiment)
Mills, F	Queen's Own (Royal West Kent Regiment)
Moon, A C	Royal Navy
Murray, E F	London Regiment (Artists' Rifles)
Naughton, V S G	London Regiment (Post Office Rifles)
Naylor, E C	The Queen's (Royal West Surrey Regiment)
Neville, H L	Middlesex Regiment

Norley, L G	Australian Field Artillery
Norris, W E	Royal Sussex Regiment
Obee, S T	Northumberland Fusiliers
Page, A W	Queen's Own (Royal West Kent Regiment)
Parker, C	Hampshire Regiment
Parker, E S	The Queen's (Royal West Surrey Regiment)
Parker, S	The Buffs (East Kent Regiment)
Parslow, F D	Royal Engineers
Payling, A E	New Zealand Field Artillery
Pearce, E E	London Regiment
Pearce, G A	Royal Naval Reserve
Peen, J R	Royal Sussex Regiment
Perrin, I J	East Surrey Regiment
Pett, A	Queen's Own (Royal West Kent Regiment)
Phillips, A L	Mercantile Marine
Phipps, E W	The Buffs (East Kent Regiment)
Pound, R	Machine Gun Corps (Infantry)
Pratt, S A	Royal Navy (HMS *Cornwallis*)
Prince, P O	The Buffs (East Kent Regiment)
Pryer, F A	Queen's Own (Royal West Kent Regiment)
Puzey, C C	South African Horse
Raggatt, S T	Royal Garrison Artillery
Reffell, G S	Queen's Own (Royal West Kent Regiment)
Relf, R	Royal Field Artillery
Reynolds, H R	Royal Navy (HMS *Torrent*)
Richardson, J	South Wales Borderers
Robinson, W G	Queen's Own (Royal West Kent Regiment)
Robus, T J	Royal Engineers
Roots, C G	Middlesex Regiment
Ruck, E W	Queen's Own (Royal West Kent Regiment)
Sage, V	The Buffs (East Kent Regiment)
Saunders, A	Machine Gun Corps (Infantry)
Saunders, F H	Queen's Own (Royal West Kent Regiment)
Sayer, R B	Royal Fusiliers
Scherf, O L	The Buffs (East Kent Regiment)
Sellen, C L	Queen's Own (Royal West Kent Regiment)

Selves, W	Royal Warwickshire Regiment
Senior, J	Northumberland Fusiliers
Short, W J	Royal Army Medical Corps
Simmons, E G	Queen's Own (Royal West Kent Regiment)
Singyard, E	Queen's Own (Royal West Kent Regiment)
Smissen, W J	Royal Navy (HMS *Calypso*)
Smith, E G	Welsh Regiment
Smith, G T	Suffolk Regiment
Smith, M	Queen's Own (Royal West Kent Regiment)
Smith, N	Queen's Own (Royal West Kent Regiment)
Springett, E S	1st Canadian Mounted Rifles
Standbridge, F J	Royal Army Medical Corps
Starke, D R V	London Regiment (Queen's Westminster Rifles)
Startup, L	Northumberland Fusiliers
Steel, T C	Bedfordshire Regiment
Stevens, C P	Middlesex Regiment
Stevens, P J	Queen's Own (Royal West Kent Regiment)
Stevenson, A L	Royal Sussex Regiment
Terry, F H	The Buffs (East Kent Regiment)
Terry, H	The Buffs (East Kent Regiment)
Thomas, L A	Royal Army Medical Corps
Thompson, F	London Regiment (Royal Fusiliers)
Thompson, W	Queen's Own (Royal West Kent Regiment)
Thorpe, A E	Grenadier Guards
Tolhurst, F B	London Regiment (London Rifle Brigade)
Tomkin, P	Royal Navy (HMS *Hannibal*)
Tomsett, E A	Queen's Own (Royal West Kent Regiment)
Tonybee, A	Mercantile Marine
Trousdell, M G	Army Service Corps
Turrell, T	South Staffordshire Regiment
Underdown, J T	Royal Berkshire Regiment
Venton, F	The Buffs (East Kent Regiment)
Waghorne, C F	12th (Prince of Wales Royal) Lancers
Walker, H E	Coldstream Guards
Wallond, G G	Army Service Corps

Walter, S R P — Royal Flying Corps
Waterman, E R — Queen's Own (Royal West Kent Regiment)
Watson, A S — Royal Navy (HMS *Vanguard*)
Watt, W H — Australian Infantry
Wells, W F — Grenadier Guards
West, W J — Queen's Own (Royal West Kent Regiment)
Wheeler, A — Queen's Own (Royal West Kent Regiment)
White, H B — Royal Field Artillery
White, T W — East Surrey Regiment
Whitehead, W L — The King's (Liverpool Regiment)
Wightwick, E B — Royal Sussex Regiment
Williams, E — Royal Fusiliers
Williams, F S — Sherwood Foresters (Notts & Derby Regiment)
Willmore, A — Machine Gun Corps (Infantry)
Winch, J — King's Royal Rifle Corps
Winchester, J — Middlesex Regiment
Wisdom, A J — Royal Naval Volunteer Reserve
Woodley, W H — Cheshire Regiment
Woolven, F — The Queen's (Royal West Surrey Regiment)
Wright, A B — West Yorkshire Regiment (Prince of Wales Own)
Wynn, R C — Australian Infantry
Yorke, E — Queen's Own (Royal West Kent Regiment)

1918

Adams, P — Royal Garrison Artillery
Adams, C J N — Grenadier Guards
Allcorn, R — Queen's Own (Royal West Kent)
Allen, J A — South Staffordshire Regiment
Anderton, A — Royal Field Artillery
Ashdown, H G — The King's (Liverpool Regiment)
Austin, A — Queen's Own (Royal West Kent Regiment)
Avery, H E — Army Service Corps
Baker, F H — Queen's Own (Royal West Kent Regiment)
Ball, A J — London Regiment (First Surrey Rifles)

Ballard, R E	Bedfordshire Regiment
Barnes, C S	Army Service Corps
Baxter, P W	East Surrey Regiment
Beasley, A W	Army Service Corps
Beer, C W	Royal Fusiliers
Bennett, F	Canadian Infantry
Betts, J P	The Buffs (East Kent Regiment)
Blackman, C	Queen's Own (Royal West Kent Regiment)
Blundell, R V	Queen's Own (Royal West Kent Regiment)
Body, J G	Suffolk Regiment
Bony, S	Northumberland Fusiliers
Bony, A E	Army Service Corps
Bowden, A J	Royal Garrison Artillery
Bowles, J	Australian Infantry
Branscombe, J T	Machine Gun Corps (Infantry)
Bratton, A A	Royal Inniskilling Fusiliers
Bridger, H E	Gloucestershire Regiment
Britcher, J J F	Queen's Own (Royal West Kent Regiment)
Brown, S C	Royal Engineers
Brown, T	Royal Field Artillery
Budd, J H	Royal Garrison Artillery
Bugden, C W	Leicestershire Regiment
Burt, G B	Royal Field Artillery
Candler, A E	Canadian Infantry
Carter, W E J	Queen's Own (Royal West Kent Regiment)
Chambers, C	Machine Gun Corps (Infantry)
Chapman, A	East Lancashire Regiment
Chapman, H J	Queen's Own (Royal West Kent Regiment)
Chapman, R L	Royal Munster Fusiliers
Clark, F G	Queen's Own (Royal West Kent Regiment)
Clark, W G	Royal Sussex Regiment
Cogger, C A	Royal Fusiliers
Coleman, E	North Staffordshire Regiment
Collier, W	Army Service Corps
Cook, L J	London Regiment
Cooper, L	Queen's Own (Royal West Kent Regiment)

Coster, C V	Machine Gun Corps, (Cavalry)
Coulter, C W	Royal Engineers
Court, A W	Royal Navy (HMS *Victory*)
Cox, G D	Machine Gun Corps (Infantry)
Craddock, W	Royal Australian Navy (HMAS *Barambah*)
Cronk, A	Royal Fusiliers
Cronk, A	London Regiment (London Irish Rifles)
Croucher, W	Essex Regiment
Cruttenden, F	South Wales Borderers
Cushion, A C	King's Own Scottish Borderers
Dann, L J	Royal Army Medical Corps
Davis, F L	New Zealand Rifle Brigade
Davis, W H	Queen's Own (Royal West Kent Regiment)
Dodge, W	Royal Navy (HMS *Pembroke*)
Dunmall, P R	Royal Field Artillery
Dunmill, J B	Royal Garrison Artillery
Durrant, L	The Buffs (East Kent Regiment)
Edmett, A W	Queen's Own (Royal West Kent Regiment)
Edmunds, F W	Queen's Own (Royal West Kent Regiment)
Edwards, A T B	Rifle Brigade
Elliot, H N	Lancashire Fusiliers
Emery, J H	Royal Army Medical Corps
Eversfield, W L	Machine Gun Corps
Farley, J E	Bedfordshire Regiment
Featherstone, R E	Royal Garrison Artillery
Fenton, W H	Machine Gun Corps (Cavalry)
Fishenden, H A	Royal Naval Volunteer Reserve (HMS *Racoon*)
Ford, C F	The Buffs (East Kent Regiment)
Foreman, L S	Queen's Own (Royal West Kent Regiment)
Fry, W D	Gloucestershire Regiment
Gardener, W	Queen's Own (Royal West Kent Regiment)
Gardner, W	Royal Navy (HMS *Raglan*)
Gibson, R H	Royal Warwickshire Regiment
Giles, L	Middlesex Regiment
Gill, E H H	Royal Air Force

Glendinning, W L	Canadian Infantry
Goodbody, S R	Mercantile Marine
Green, E	Gloucestershire Regiment
Green, L V	Tank Corps
Greenaway, A	Royal Army Medical Corps
Grundtvig, H H	Leicestershire Regiment
Hadaway, C H	Royal Field Artillery
Hamnett, F G	King's Royal Rifle Corps
Harding, A K	Queen's Own (Royal West Kent Regiment)
Harris, R H	Machine Gun Corps (Infantry)
Hawkins, K E	Royal Fusiliers
Hawks, H J	South Staffordshire Regiment
Head, R	Queen's Own (Royal West Kent Regiment)
Hendley, F	Royal Field Artillery
Henniker, E	Royal Sussex Regiment
Henty, R	Royal Field Artillery
Hicks, C	The Buffs (East Kent Regiment)
Hills, J	Machine Gun Corps
Hinkley, H	Royal Field Artillery
Hoar, E	Canadian infantry
Hodges, G H	Royal Army Medical Corps
Hodgkin, T	Grenadier Guards
Hodgson, H	Australian Infantry
Hook, F W	Canadian Infantry
Hoole, F S W	Mercantile Marine
Horton, A E	Royal Army Medical Corps
Howard, H	Seaforth Highlanders
Howard, J A	Army Service Corps
Hubble, F R	Army Service Corps
Hughes, G W	Machine Gun Corps (Infantry)
Iles, J	Royal Fusiliers
Johnson, F	Royal Fusiliers
Jones, C E	Royal Field Artillery
Jones, G	Duke of Cornwall's Light Infantry
King, D A	Royal Sussex Regiment
Kingsley, J	Australian Infantry

Knell, F H	Royal Fusiliers
Lacey, A W	Army Pay Corps
Lamb, W J	Norfolk Regiment
Langdon, J E	Machine Gun Corps (Infantry)
Larkin, H	Royal Air Force
Latter, A	Bedfordshire Regiment
Latter, J	King's Shropshire Light Infantry
Laurence, R	Canadian Infantry
Leney, B	Royal Field Artillery
Leonard, C E	Royal Engineers
Letts, H C	Royal Engineers
Longley, F E	The Buffs (East Kent Regiment)
Maidstone, A V	Royal Warwickshire Regiment
Mankee, A H	Essex Regiment
Mankelow, H C	Queen's Own (Royal West Kent Regiment)
Mann, C E	Bedfordshire Regiment
Mannerings, E	Norfolk Regiment
Manning, A	Queen's Own (Royal West Kent Regiment)
Marchant, R F J	Queen's Own (Royal West Kent Regiment)
Martin, A R	Tank Corps
Martin, J A W	London Regiment (City of London Rifles)
Martin, J F A	Queen's Own (Royal West Kent Regiment)
Martin, W B	Canadian Infantry
Maskell, J W	Royal Engineers
Mason, A G	Royal Garrison Artillery
Maynard, W E	Army Service Corps
McLellan, D C	Royal Field Artillery
McLeod, A	Royal Field Artillery
McNeil, A J	Cheshire Regiment
Meopham, A A E	Machine Gun Corps (Infantry)
Merralls, W G	London Regiment (First Surrey Rifles)
Mills, E T	Queen's Own (Royal West Kent Regiment)
Moon, F H	The Queen's (Royal West Surrey Regiment)
Morling, H	Army Service Corps
Moseley, F J	Queen's Own (Royal West Kent Regiment)
Mummery, H N S	Highland Light Infantry

Neeves, W	Royal Air Force
Newing, E T	South Staffordshire Regiment
Newing, R	North Staffordshire Regiment
Onions, J F	Royal Engineers
Osborne, J	Royal Naval Volunteer Reserve
Page, A E	Bedfordshire Regiment
Paine, E J	Royal Engineers
Partridge, R H	Royal Navy (HMS *Cassandra*)
Pattenden, H R	Seaforth Highlanders
Pattison, H J	East Surrey Regiment
Payne, L W	London Regiment (Royal Fusiliers)
Pearce, F E	Royal Engineers
Pearce, H	Worcestershire Regiment
Pearce, R	Royal Air Force
Pearson, A E	Queen's Own (Royal West Kent Regiment)
Pearson, W	Royal Army Medical Corps
Perrin, H	Middlesex Regiment
Pettitt, H J	Royal Army Medical Corps
Philpott, C E	Herefordshire Regiment
Price, H C J	Lincolnshire Regiment
Raggatt, E C	Royal Engineers
Ranger, T R	King's Own Yorkshire Light Infantry
Rasey, T P	Queen's Own (Royal West Kent Regiment)
Reason, G F	East Yorkshire Regiment
Reynolds, G W	Royal Garrison Artillery
Richardson, G W	Queen's Own (Royal West Kent Regiment)
Richmond, S R	Royal Air Force
Ring, W	South Wales Borderers
Rogers, H G	Queen's Own (Royal West Kent Regiment)
Rogers, L J	Royal Field Artillery
Rose, F E	4th (Queen's Own) Hussars
Russell, W C	Hampshire Regiment
Sage, H V	Essex Regiment
Savage, R J	The Buffs (East Kent Regiment)
Savage, W J	Suffolk Regiment
Scott, W E	Royal Marine Light Infantry

Scudder, A G	Middlesex Regiment
Sharp, A V	East Surrey Regiment
Sheppard, G F	New Zealand Service Corps
Skinner, F	Queen's Own (Royal West Kent Regiment)
Smith, A	Suffolk Regiment
Smith, F	The Buffs (East Kent Regiment)
Smith, G	East Surrey Regiment
Smith, W G T	Gloucestershire Regiment
Snashall, H	Royal Navy (HMS *Wildfire*)
Solley, A C	South Nottinghamshire Hussars
Spice, E J	Royal Fusiliers
Standen, T	Queen's Own (Royal West Kent Regiment)
Stansell, L B	Royal Air Force
Stocker, C T F	Royal Sussex Regiment
Stubbs, W F E	Sherwood Foresters (Notts & Derby Regiment)
Swaffer, W G	Royal Field Artillery
Sykes, J A	Royal Air Force
Theobald, R	Suffolk Regiment
Tickner, M E	Royal Fusiliers
Tilbrook, A J	King's Royal Rifle Corps
Tompsett, F J	Royal Army Service Corps
Tong, A F	Royal Air Force
Town, W	Royal Garrison Artillery
Tree, W	Royal Army Service Corps
Trodd, J R	Sherwood Foresters (Notts & Derby Regiment)
Tye, P S	North Staffordshire Regiment
Underdown, A E T	North Staffordshire Regiment
Underwood, H C	Irish Guards
Unwin, F G	Middlesex Regiment
Waghorn, C A	Royal Warwickshire Regiment
Waghorne, W T H	Northumberland Fusiliers
Wakefield, R	King's Royal Rifle Corps
Walmsley, H S	Royal Air Force
Ware, G	The Buffs (East Kent Regiment)

Warner, C F S	Northamptonshire Regiment
Waterman, A E	Bedfordshire Regiment
Watkins, L	Queen's Own (Royal West Kent Regiment)
Watson, W E	South Staffordshire Regiment
Wellard, C W	Middlesex Regiment
Wenham, A C	Royal Fusiliers
West, L	Seaforth Highlanders
White, E A	Royal Fusiliers
Williams, W A J	King's Royal Rifle Corps
Wissenden, H S	Army Service Corps
Wolford, W F	Royal Garrison Artillery
Woodhams, H	Royal Berkshire Regiment

1919

Agland, S	Royal Garrison Artillery
Allcorn, G C	Royal Army Service Corps
Ashby, A E	Royal Army Medical Corps
Austin, E G	Royal Horse Artillery
Caney, W	Royal Fusiliers
Canton, H	King's Royal Rifle Corps
Capeling, J W	The Queen's (Royal West Surrey Regiment)
Chambers, C V	Durham Light Infantry
Dann, S W J	Royal Engineers
Harfleet, F G	Royal Army Medical Corps
Hayes, W H	Royal Engineers
Iliffe, H	Queen's Own (Royal West Kent Regiment)
Latter, E F	Queen's Own (Royal West Kent Regiment)
Laurence, M	Royal Army Service Corps
Leavey, D	London Regiment
McVicar, W	Machine Gun Corps (Infantry)
Mitchell, C	Rifle Brigade
Prior, R W	Canadian Corps Cyclist Battalion
Sudds, H L	Royal Sussex Regiment
Wadkinson, R A	Queen's Own (Royal West Kent Regiment)
Wakefield, J E	Territorial Force Nursing Service
Wilkinson, J H	Royal Canadian Regiment

1920

Johnston, E S	Royal Garrison Artillery
Manuell, C E	Royal Horse Artillery
Toms, E A	Royal Field Artillery

1921

Cornwallis, F W M	17th Lancers (Duke of Cambridge's Own)
Glover, L	Tank Corps
Hagon, G W	Essex Regiment

The first 'Maidstone' man to be killed in the fighting of the First World War was 21-year-old Arthur Henry Walliker. At the time, Arthur's parents, Arthur and Emily, lived at 20 Charles Street in the town. But Arthur wasn't born there. He hailed from Slough in Buckinghamshire. The 1901 census shows the family living in Slough, Buckinghamshire and in 1911 them living in Epsom in Surrey. Arthur was a private (10153) in the 1st Battalion, East Surrey Regiment, which he had joined in 1911 after his 18th birthday. He was killed in fighting during the retreat from Mons on 23 August 1914, having only arrived in Belgium a week earlier. He is buried at the Hautrage Military Cemetery, in the Hainault region of Belgium. The cemetery was actually begun by the Germans in August 1914.

To show how difficult it can be to establish a fact beyond all reasonable doubt in relation to the First World War, I have looked at the second 'Maidstone' man to lose his life during the First World War. This was Robert Banks, who the Commonwealth War Graves Commission website shows as being 26 years of age and a private (L/7676) in the First Battalion, Queen's Own (Royal West Kent Regiment). The website records that he was killed in action on 24 August 1914 and that his name is commemorated on the La Ferté-sous-Jouarre memorial in Seine-et-Marne. His wife, Edith Clare Banks, is shown as living at 149 Bower Street, Maidstone, but I have not been able to establish a direct connection between Robert and Maidstone. The British Army's Medal Rolls cards index for the period that covers the First World War shows that he was killed on 28 October 1914 and not in August. This is definitely the same man, but as can be seen, confusion reigns.

Below are the figures for the number of 'Maidstone' men who were killed during each of the war years. These numbers also include those who died of their wounds or illness up to the end of 1921:

1914 – 56
1915 – 122
1916 – 194
1917 – 263
1918 – 235
1919 – 22
1920 – 3
1921 – 3

These figures clearly show that the peak year in which these 'Maidstone' men died was 1917, when 263 of them lost their lives fighting for King and country. As best as I have been able to establish, and I by no means suggest that it is a one hundred per cent definitive figure, 896 men and 2 women lost their lives as a result of being in some kind of military related service during the First World War.

Although 'Maidstone' men, they collectively served in over one hundred different Corps or Regiments from across the Commonwealth.

The two women were Una Marguerite Duncanson, a nurse with the Voluntary Aid Detachment. She was killed on New Year's Eve 1917 when the ship she was on, HMS *Osmanieh*, struck a mine while entering the harbour at Alexandria in Egypt. Una, along with 198 others who were on board at the time, sadly lost their lives in the tragedy. She is buried at the Hadra Military Cemetery in Alexandria. Two of Una's brothers were also killed during the war.

The other woman was Jessie Emily Wakefield, who was a nursing sister with the Territorial Nursing Service. She died of illness on 7 February 1919 while serving in France and is buried at the Étaples Military Cemetery.

There are at least fifty-eight other war memorials or rolls of honour scattered throughout the Maidstone area. Included in these pages are just a few of them.

The Memorial for the Queen's Own (Royal West Kent Regiment), was unveiled on 30 July 1921.

Royal West Kent Regiment Memorial.

Hollingbourne War Memorial.

Maidstone – Hollingbourne

The village of Hollingbourne is situated about four miles to the east of Maidstone. There are thirty-seven names on the Hollingbourne Roll of Honour of the men who lost their lives during the First World War. They are as follows:

Henry Barling
William Clackett
William John Cleggett
Albert Edward Croucher
Leslie Stephen Court
William Curtis
Frederick Day
Hugh Russell Elliot
Arthur Robert Felton
F Foster
Walter Dannial Fry
Fred Gatland

Charles Gibson
F Godrey
Walter Bousfield Watkins Grubbs
Arthur Frederick Hawkins
Leonard Ingram
Robert Mellor
Walter Edmund Jordan
Alfred Albert Kite
Alfred McLean
Victor Philpott
Stanley Theodore Overell Rugg
William Henry Rutley
Albert Sands
George Seymour
George Smith
George William Stevenson
William Amos Summers
Ernest Alfred Tomsett
Walter Herbert Ward
Robert William Watts
Reginald Weaver
Charles Weekes
William Albert Winter
George Winder
Wood

There is also the Hollingbourne War Memorial, which is in the shape of a cross and was erected in Eyhorne Street and unveiled on 15 April 1922.

Maidstone – St. Faiths Church

The Roll of Honour at St. Faiths Church in Maidstone is representative of churches up and down the country who have Rolls of Honour, plaques and other similar memorials adorning their walls to remember and commemorate the lives of their parishioners. At the time of the First World War religion was a big part of everyday life. The church was the centre of every community and everybody went there every Sunday morning. If somebody didn't attend Sunday church it was not only noticed, but questions would be asked and the vicar would make a visit to their home to find out what was wrong. There are twenty-three names commemorated on the Roll of Honour in St. Faiths. Where possible, I have included their addresses.

In most grateful memory
Of all those of St. Faith's who
Died for the cause of
Liberty & Justice
in the Great War, 1914-1919

Ethelbert George Anderson (11 Sheals Crescent)
William Leslie Baker (93 King Road)
Wallace J Baker
Malcolm A Baskett ('Roseville', 6 Buckland Hill)
Edward Victor Bonner (10 Waterside)
Frank Victor Bridges (14 Waterside)
George Burgess
William T Caney (13 Fairmeadow)
William Henry Davis (65 Week Street)
Albert C Harris
Roland Hibbin (52 Salisbury Road)
George H Hodges (4 Dann's Cottage, High Street)
Alfred Holmes (38 Allen Street)
Albert Alfred Marchant (32 Faith Street)
Frank Auger Pryer (12 Medway Terrace)
Frank Pullen (209 Loose Road)
Lionel Brough Stansell (MM) (17 Albion Place)
Thomas C Steel (5 Upper Rant Road)
Horace Terry (6 Dann's Cottages, High Street)
Frederick John Towner (60 Earl Street)
Percy Thomas Winchester (10 Market Street)
Herbert S Wissenden (93A Week Street)
Sister Jessie Emily Wakefield (27 Mote Road)

The final chapter is always the most poignant because it is about those who died, those who never came home, those who never got to see and hold their loved ones ever again. Even the brave deeds that many of them carried out during the war are overshadowed by their passing, which didn't make the suffering of their loved ones, any less painful.

It wasn't a Great War, it was bloody and brutal, a war that killed millions of people. It wasn't the war to end all wars and the phrase, 'he died a glorious death' isn't very helpful to anybody. We should honour those who fought and died, that is only right and proper, but war itself shouldn't be glorified, because ultimately it is just legalized murder.

Conclusion

With the signing of the armistice the war was finally over, but life as everyone had known it before was never to be quite the same again. The war had taken a great toll on all those concerned. People had been killed, families had grieved, countries had mourned; the peace had been hard won and came at a great price. Young men had paid their dues and earned the right to expect a better life for themselves and their families. The men of Britain, the Commonwealth and their Allies had kept their end of the bargain, they had fought and won the war with their blood sweat and tears. Now that the guns were silenced and the war was over, it was down to the politicians to manage the peace. Only time would tell if it had all been worthwhile.

As for Maidstone, like other towns, cities and villages up and down the country, life began to return to a form of normality. Men returned to the town either as able-bodied returning soldiers, released prisoners of war, or wounded men who needed time for their scars to heal, some of which were mental rather than physical. In some cases, people had to get to know their own families again, having not seen each other for years. Many wives had become independent through their wartime work, which they now didn't want to give up. Children had grown up over the four and half years of war, some having never seen their fathers before. Most of the men never spoke about their wartime experiences, the memories were too painful and traumatic.

The overriding feeling was a sense of togetherness in the journey ahead, on the path to a brighter future and a better tomorrow.

Sources

Ian Castle & Christa Hook, *London 1914-1917: The Zeppelin Menace* (2008)
The archivist, Maidstone Grammar School
ancestry.co.uk
britishnewspaperarchive.co.uk
cwgc.org.uk
flightglobal.com
hollingbournepc.kentparishes.gov.uk
hut-six.co.uk
kentfallen.com
kenthistoryforum.co.uk
kentvad.org
longlongtrail.co.uk
redcross.org.uk
spartacus-education.com
wartimememoriesproject.com
wikipedia.com
ww1centenary.oucs.ox.ac.uk

Index